SUSPECT TENDERNESS

MAN IS MORE

than a face his father yearned
over still waters. Behind that irony
carved and enclosed, soul
is personal diamond: into dark says:
stars are more than dark refuses them.

Man is more than day denies him:
all things of stone or music, setting against time
a living shoulder, a flower's stubborn
delicacy.

Soul is a soul changed
in mid-journey to nightingale:
it sits the golden bough, unreels its voice
for even as us: I am wronged
but not silenced: I pour my light, my coals
upon just and guilty. Bear it
who can.

The dancer improvises and is hardly there:
a whirling diamond: each attitude
a universe. Our hearts cry
sensing through ease that agony: be still.
One could as well halt the heart cold.
No: he must mime life to life again.

Not invisible, but strictly contained. You must
keep vigil, not be above
lowly unexpected showings. I see him
in shape of hand, cleave and bid aside
the dark. Or with password friend pass
in another's eyes. Suspect tenderness
of harboring him.

DANIEL BERRIGAN, S.J.

SUSPECT TENDERNESS

The Ethics of the Berrigan Witness

By WILLIAM STRINGFELLOW
and ANTHONY TOWNE

with a Preface by DANIEL BERRIGAN, S.J.
FEDERAL PRISONER #23742-145

HOLT, RINEHART AND WINSTON
New York, Chicago, San Francisco

ISBN: 0-03-086581-6

Library of Congress Catalog Card Number: 74-155534

First Edition

Designer: A. Christopher Simon

PRINTED IN THE UNITED STATES OF AMERICA

21976

CONTENTS

III
CONSCIENCE, TACTICS, AND HOPE   *95*

IV
DOCUMENTS OF THE BLOCK ISLAND CASE   *115*

FOREWORD

Conventional prudence argues against writing and publishing this book because it admires and commends the public witness of the Berrigan brothers against the war establishment in America, against the totalitarianization of society and, most basically, against death as the dominating American social purpose.

By speaking out at all about the issues which Daniel and Philip have been confronting and dramatizing, or about the offenses for which both of them have been consigned to prison, or about further charges uttered against them, we call attention both to the Berrigan witness—which the public authorities are said variously to desire to discredit, suppress, or minimize—and to our longstanding friendship for these priests, especially our hospitality to Daniel while he remained a fugitive and the fact of his capture at our home on Block Island on August 11,

1970. The implication is that public mention of these matters by us risks reprisal from the State against us. A great many persons put just such a construction upon the indictment procured by the federal authorities against us on December 17, 1970, charging us with harboring and concealing Daniel Berrigan so as to prevent his discovery and arrest and with being accessories after the fact of the offenses committed by Daniel Berrigan at Catonsville, Maryland, in the spring of 1968, by relieving, receiving, comforting, and assisting him "in order to prevent and hinder his punishment" by offering and giving sustenance and lodging to him. We have both long since abandoned speculation about why we were thus indicted or, for that matter, we have also given up second-guessing what— in a broader context—motivates the incumbent administration in the Justice Department. Such speculation ends, we observe, in a dissipation of intelligence and common sense. While, at the time we were indicted, we made notice of "the pervasiveness of the spirit of repression which has lately overtaken the nation," we knew well our innocence of the charges made against us, or of any other offense, and we therefore kept trust that thorough and honest inquiry and due process of law would verify that the charges had no basis in fact or in law. As far as we are concerned, the dismissal of the indictment on February 16, 1971, in the United States District Court for Rhode Island, redeems that trust.

In the circumstances—if anything—it seems to us that our ordeal renders an enhanced obligation as citizens, as well as a definite responsibility as Christians, to speak out in this society at this time. Yet, in the aftermath of the dismissal, silence as a caution against real or fancied reprisal risks has been more strenuously urged upon us than ever before. What accounts for this apprehensiveness on the part of many citizens toward the State, we do not precisely know; doubtless it has multifarious origins. The documentation in the hearings over which Senator Sam Ervin presided in February, 1971, of the ubiquity of official—if illegal—surveillance of citizens in the exercise of their elementary Constitutional rights appears relevant. The exceptional pressures to conform the public media to the administration's version of events, particularly those pertaining to the Indochina war, and specifically in circumstances where the government's account is unworthy of credibility, are also pertinent. And, in the interval between indictment and dismissal in our case, there have been notorious developments respecting the Berrigan brothers in the utterance of what seem to us to be truly fantastic allegations of a scheme to kidnap Dr. Strangelove himself. Such incidents as these may have scared many citizens and inspired in them the view that silence is prudence.

Though deemed prudential, we find this counsel of quietism of alien circular logic. It posits fear as the primary reality in the relationship between citizen and government. It presupposes that, in these days in America, charges are published, indictments are procured, prosecutions are pursued out of political motives, irrationality, and other delicate influences, rather than according to the law, the facts, and rational judgment. Thus silence is supposed to be the safest conduct. What historical verdict may one day be rendered on the extent to which the operation of the legal system has been politicized in this manner at the present time, we venture no predictions. But we maintain a moral certainty that silence is no safety. The experiences of many colleagues, friends, and fellow Christians—like Alan Paton, Martin Niemöller, Jacques Ellul—in situations elsewhere with which the contemporary American scene justifies comparisons—have been edifying to that extent at least.

We have suffered, for that matter, because of our friendship for Dan Berrigan, a surveillance by the authorities and have found that when one is constantly and closely spied upon or overheard it becomes a temptation to imagine that one really does have something to hide. It is an insidious game, suited only to totalitarianism. We have no reason to be silent and, indeed, we have specific grounds to speak, to write, to publish. Quietism in this society is radically irresponsible: it instigates and sponsors the very intimidation of life against which it claims precaution. Silence conjures up repression; speaking out may be an exorcism.

This book has four main sections. The first, "On Sheltering Criminal Priests," is a narrative concerning the capture of Daniel Berrigan, related in the context of our continuing friendship and mutual pastoral relationships. Next are four pieces which explore theological implications of the Berrigan witness. In each instance, these originated in immediate circumstances where there was reason to try to probe and explicate the theological and, particularly, biblical connections pertinent to the witness of the Berrigans. Of the four, the one entitled "Jesus as a Criminal" was first given as a sermon at Cornell University in October of 1969, at a service at which Daniel Berrigan was the liturgist, he then being free on bond pending appeal of the case of the Catonsville Nine. The other three, in their initial versions, each done shortly after Dan's capture, were also addressed to particular congregations or audiences: "An Authority Over Death" at St. John's Episcopal Church, Northampton, Massachusetts (the hometown parish of Stringfellow); "Who Are the Prisoners?" at a mass for prisoners of conscience at St. Clement's Church, New York City; "The State, the Church, and the Reality of Conscience" as a paper for the Canon Law Society of America. The third part, entitled "Conscience, Tactics, and Hope" seeks to examine the theological meaning of conscience and to suggest a concrete relationship of ethics, action, and eschatology. The final section continues, as it were, the narrative of the first part by publishing the documents of our indictment and the dismissal of that case and, thus, allowing the documents in the case to speak for themselves without editorialization from either of us.

Our comments on the Block Island case and on some of the issues of continuing involvement in this society are set forth here in a public letter which we jointly wrote to the Berrigan brothers at the prison in Danbury some weeks after the dismissal of charges against us.

Sometime after Dan Berrigan was imprisoned, there came to our attention an extraordinary tape he had made while he was a fugitive. It is a sermon. He had furnished it to the Chaplain of Smith College to be played at a service there in lieu of his personal appearance. We regard it as a brilliant exposition of his situation—and of the nation's moral crisis— and as a document of the biblical spirit which fundamentally informs the Berrigan witness, and we gratefully publish it here as a preface.

We share the responsibility for this book, though parts of it, as is self-evident, have been written by one or the other of us.

WILLIAM STRINGFELLOW
ANTHONY TOWNE

Eschaton
Block Island, Rhode Island
Saturday Next Before Palm Sunday, 1971

A Christian does what he must do as a Christian.

*Daniel Berrigan is our friend and is always welcome in our home.
Any visit from him is an honor for us because he is a priest of
uncommon conscience, he is a citizen of urgent moral purpose, and
he is a human being of exemplary courage.**

WILLIAM STRINGFELLOW

ANTHONY TOWNE

* Statement issued by the authors on August 11, 1970, after federal
authorities seized Father Berrigan at their home on Block Island, R.I.

PREFACE

A HOMILY BY A FUGITIVE PRIEST

by DANIEL BERRIGAN, S.J.

Dear friends, this is Father Daniel Berrigan speaking. I might say, speaking from the Underground. I want to greet many old and new friends, as well as to express regret at not being able to be with you for your worship. By way of consolation, I can at least think of you and pray with you as you gather in Christ's name.

In times such as we are enduring, it seems necessary above all else, I think, to allow the Word of God full play in our lives and our minds. For myself, I know beyond any doubt that I must sink or swim by virtue of a very simple act of faith, drawn from our Testament. For my present, as you must know, is obscure to the point of darkness. I have no real

3

idea of what my Underground state may mean for others, where it is meant to lead me, or what contribution it may be supposed to make for peace, for justice among men. As far as the future is concerned, that is all too clear. It means for me the fate of my brother Philip, already entered upon, as well as the fate of so many friends who are paying a very heavy price for an equivalent witness.

Well, if I bring all of this up before you, it is not, dear friends, in order to wage an assault upon your compassion. It is merely to share with you one Christian's understanding of what the faith is exacting in these times. For I think this is always the burden of such times as we are enduring—the faith which is at once dark, and yet undeniable and clear in its demands; which is costly, and yet is generous in its return upon us; which is the call of a jealous God upon his sons, and yet a love of that prodigal Father returned to us a hundredfold.

But what is it like, practically speaking, to live as I do these days? To try to be faithful day after day to those demands that are made upon one? To believe, to believe simply in the breach? Or as a young resister put it to me recently, "What does the Underground do to your head?"

You know, it was strange, but that question came to me with something of a shock. I had not thought of this decision of mine, of this style or direction as something that might possibly be deranging to my purported sanity. No, I had taken my choice in a clumsy, unformulated way. I had judged that it was in a sense self-evident that one's head could only benefit by such a move as mine, attempting, as I did, literally to use my head, to weigh the evidence on the war, on national policy, on the crossing of frontiers, especially on the continuing death game of the nation, a game that continued whether the losers were to be Cambodians or Panthers or students or resisters or, finally, clerics themselves. Well, I assure you, as I tried to assure my young friend, that my head is in good order. I am able to face the facts of life and death.

They include, undeniably, the fact that my brother is in prison, that I will eventually go to prison, that our lives are sharing in some small degree in the suffering dislocation of our brothers across the world. Which is to say, simply, that things with us are normal. They are, we believe, as they should be—insofar, that is, as we allow the grace of Christ full play in hand and heart, and do not block his will with our willfulness.

But I don't want to lose my original intent here. I began by suggesting that it is in the Word of God one finds the resources to keep going in such times as these. I have been asking myself in prayer, asking the Lord for a clue as to the meaning of this strange existence I am leading. I would like to share with you a few insights that the past months have granted me.

It seems to me that we start with a literal fact. The "Underground" is a kind of rehearsal, a metaphor I think, for Death itself. It is in that Underground that man is literally ground under. Dust to dust, we are told. Prison, of course, is another such image. So is illness, serious incapacity, so is poverty, so is race in a racist state.

But I think what makes this metaphor of particular interest to me is that nonviolent life outside the law—a definition of the Underground as I see it—is a kind of life outside the law of Death itself. I hope this sentence is not too complicated. We can put the same thing another way. By becoming an outlaw, I am seeking to outlaw Death. This, I think, is an insight our Testament grants us. I think this is one way of putting the Savior's view of his own life. That reign of Death he saw as all but universal, all but omnipotent, all but omnivorous, carnivorous in its intention and method, claiming all flesh for itself. No one, but no one, could stand aside from those claims or show cause for exemption from Death; no one, not in all our history.

Death is even a kind of universal military service, debasing to the free will of men and to God's intent for life. It mobilizes

every man and woman born. To die, not to live—a formula
which puts Death simply where it belongs: in direct and willed
antithesis and conflict with the Will of God in our regard.

Now suppose for a moment, as indeed I think our Savior
supposed, that one finds the presumptions of Death presump-
tuous. Suppose one wishes to play another game. Suppose the
implications of the Death game stink in one's nostrils, with
all their assorted smells and whiffs of duplicity, of political
corruption, or promises broken, and life destroyed, and property misused, and racism encouraged, the poor benignly neglected, and the rich seated unassailably in places of power.
And religion in the midst of this game ambiguous in its own
voice, and the spiritual goods of the people diminished beyond recognition.

Supposing all this to be true, what is the tactic of the
believer? of a man? Quite simply, I think, reading the New
Testament, one says NO. Quite simply, one puts his life
where the Gospel tells him it should be, if indeed the Gospel
has something to say at all. One submits in a very true way to
Death, in order to destroy the power of Death from within.

There are, of course, as many ways of doing this as there
are men capable of opening the Book of Jesus and reading
what it says there. What our Savior says to us, it seems to me,
may be translated in many ways: as jail, as exile, as Underground, as tax-resistance, as courageous public action of any
kind which costs, which diminishes one's freedom of movement or place or action. But as the Savior reminds us, with a
certain vigor, based upon a certain unkillable vision of his
own, our reaction had better be *something*—something of
this sort. That is where you saw, as we say in the ancient
creed, "He was crucified, died, and was buried"—which is
to say he submitted before the imperial power that claimed
his life. He preferred to suffer violence in his person rather
than to inflict it on others. He died a criminal, his body placed

in a tomb. He was shoveled into the inert grave. Or as we say in the Resistance, he acted and went underground, and some days later when it was expedient for others, he surfaced again, and with great pains, identified himself as the One of the Friday we call Good.

I am struck by all this as an exemplary action and passion for ourselves. That is to say that Jesus, by a method that was breathtakingly realistic and right, sought to break the universal dominion of Death over men. Which, translated simply and historically to his times and ours, has something to do with the claims of the militaristic and imperial state, the stigma placed upon the forehead, the slaveries forged by the powerful of this world, the notion that the lives and deaths of men are the crude properties and chattels of whatever Caesar.

To confront all this, Jesus refused again and again to confront the sword with his own sword. No, he drew back from that method—that mirror game—in a gesture of ineffaceable dignity. "My kingdom," he said, "is not of this world." And to illustrate, by way of contrast, his own dynamic, he offered a figure of speech: unless the grain of wheat, falling to the ground, die, it remains alone; but if it dies, it brings forth much fruit. Here, his tactic and method are reconciled to the organic world itself in its cyclic cheating of death. Let the man who would live—die! Let him go underground if he would rise to the life of God and of mankind.

My dear friends, you recall that strange mythology that surrounds the Lord's descent into the nether regions after his death. In a place of thick shadows and encompassing darkness, spoken of by Job and the Psalmist, the early Christians saw him as rejoining the throngs of the ancient just men, awaiting through him release from Sheol. Then in the words of the primitive hymn of triumph, having rejoined his own, "captivum duxit captivitatem," a marvelously syncopated phrase which we must transliterate something like this: "He led the

enslaved free in service now only to Him." An immensely in-
triguing and powerful insight, I think. History, that is, had
become the field of force playing around the violated and
restored flesh of Jesus. Men are repulsed by those energies;
men are attracted. Slaveries are relieved or are twice forged.
Men are captive to Death or to life.

But in any case, at the very eye of history, at his immediate
hand, stand those freed from death by the man who submitted
to death in the primal image of things to come. The Underground has become the very root and spring of the Kingdom
of God. As Paul later tells us, "Sown in corruption, it is
raised in incorruption; sown in dishonor, it is raised in glory;
sown in weakness, it is raised in power."

Dear friends, I would not have any child born into this
world, into this nation, into this church, in order to bear
arms, in order to belong to the strategems of death, in order
to obey the Pentagon, in order to raven the poor in distant
lands, to die there, to kill there, in any sense, in any case, to
perish there, as man. Neither would I have any parent approve
of such disposition of the lives of others. Nor would I have
the churches support it, nor clerics remain silent before it, nor
congregations argue on its behalf. Nor would I have such a
tearing apart of the right order of things as condemns the
poor here and throughout the world to lives of utter degrada-
tion and hopelessness while we stand idly by, our ill-gotten
goods turned to weapons, our weapons turned against men.
And all this despite our Gospel and the stern claim of Christ
upon us, in life and in death.

Both my brother and myself, Philip in prison and myself in
hiding, wish that our resistance, narrowed as it is to the issue
of the war, be seen as a service for all our brothers in the
world. Indeed, we could not but wish that that service could
have taken a less obscure and anguished and ambiguous form.
We would infinitely prefer to be free, about our Father's

business, in what one might call the ordinary errands of the Gospel: to be clothing the naked, and feeding the hungry, and housing the homeless. Alas, the times are twisted. In the kingdom of Death we could not but resist Death with all our means and might.

Thus are we outlawed, forbidden free access to the community of decent men. I cannot help but reflect today how, were the promises of those in power truly kept and peace achieved in Southeast Asia, we would never need have gone to Catonsville. Or were later promises kept, and the peace at length achieved, our trial might have resulted in our vindication, as men who burned papers in protest against the burning of children. Or were the latest promises kept and the peace at last achieved, Philip and I might have submitted with good grace to prison under the greatly reduced sentences of a benign court, soon to issue again from jail with that peace which comes to hearts whose goal is achieved. Alas and alack! The promises are broken, as the lives are broken again and again. The peace is more distant than ever, drowned in the barbarism and deception and blood of the last months. In such a time the perverse logic of power dictates that men such as we must be hunted down and locked away. We, who are without weapons or riches or a stake in this world, are become a danger to the masters of the kingdom of death.

But, dear friends, if the keepers of that kingdom have their logic, so do we. We may be hunted and locked away. We will be, according to their plan. But we will also break their locks, which are the very bolts and rivets of death, for the wielders of such power are as dead to history and to mankind and to the future as any Caesar. Their claim is declared null and void by Christ himself. We are forbidden to serve in their wars. We are forbidden, that is to say, in biblical language, "to worship their gods." And as far as Philip and I are concerned, we shall never do so, so help us Christ.

May your prayers, then, follow our struggle as brethren in the Lord, and may that Lord of history and men's hearts grant you also a measure of courage and of light in perplexed and anguished times. We salute you and we thank you, with all our hearts, in Him.

ON SHELTERING CRIMINAL PRIESTS

A PRIMER FOR BIRDWATCHERS

Omens are among the several idols from which I have yet to sever my belief. Take the green parrot with the large red beak. We first saw it—William Stringfellow and I—in a pine tree outside the kitchen window from which some months later we were to remark an orange birdwatcher in a northeast storm. What was it doing, this parrot, perched on a pine tree on Block Island early in April when the mourning doves still huddled near the house for warmth? It was contemplating one of the bird feeders. That's what it was doing. But where had it come from? Inquiry about the island turned up no report of a missing parrot, but did prompt not a few suggestions that perhaps I should moderate my consumption of bourbon. Our speculations included the thought that the tropic creature had been mascot on some passing oil tanker and had escaped when the vessel paused to flush its tanks the better to pollute our beaches. But we do not know and probably will never know whence came the parrot in the pine tree. Whatever its origins, it soon established our lesser bird feeder as a place to breakfast each dawn and to supper each twilight.

Coincidental with the epiphany of green parrot arrived the news by radio of the vanishment of Daniel Berrigan, felon for peace, dear friend (buddy—as the retired bishop of South Florida might put it—in Christ). We received the news with the astonishment comparable to that we experienced on reading somewhere about Richard Nixon's fondness for cottage cheese with catsup. It was, in other words, utterly consistent with the person in question. A Christian, we have had other occasion to say, does what he must do as a Christian. Daniel Berrigan is a Christian. That he should not, in the circumstances, have vanished *would* have been an astonishment for us.

Would St. Paul, I remember asking myself, under similar circumstances—and St. Paul had, after all, *known* similar circumstances—have rendered unto Caesar that which belongs to God? Scrutiny of the Acts of the Apostles suggests that he would have done no such thing. William Buckley, the gifted dilettante conservative, in one of his columns proclaimed that Father Berrigan had refused to surrender to the state only because he did not want to go to jail. It stands as one of Mr. Buckley's least gracious and more cowardly observations. Cowardice, in this context, I take to be the imputation of base motive to someone who has performed an act one would not dare perform himself. Daniel Berrigan has, in fact, been in jail on more than one occasion during his long, fierce quest for peace and he is, in fact, now in jail for no small time. My fertile imagination is unable to summon up a series of events that would culminate in the imprisonment of William Buckley on a matter of conscience.

When the news reached us that April morning that Dan

had gone underground, had metamorphosed from felon for peace into fugitive for peace, our reflections drifted back to his several visits to Block Island, the most recent, his penultimate visit, having been in August of 1969. (To indulge fantasies that in some indeterminate future the present darkness will have lifted and further visits be entertained would be to succumb to a romantic view of history.) It had been Dan's happy custom, ever since Stringfellow and I removed ourselves to the island in 1967, to come from time to time to recuperate from his promethean encounters with the regnant principalities and powers. He seemed always to arrive in a state of exuberant exhaustion and to leave, having refreshed us gratuitously, in a state of exuberant anticipation.

One of his earlier visits had followed immediately upon an evening he had spent in the home of Sargent Shriver, an evening he had devoted to an effort to conjure up the conscience buried somewhere in the depths of Robert McNamara. No wonder he reached us in a state of exhaustion. I report this not to demean Mr. McNamara. Had the conscience not been there the effort would not have been made.

Dan's sojourns on Block Island—anywhere from a weekend to two weeks in duration—happened often enough that a liturgy for them emerged, a liturgy we followed even in his last, fugitive, and aborted sojourn. He was an easy guest to have in our home, easier than my mother, who washes dishes, irons shirts, and pastes green stamps into their prescribed wrappers. Dan did none of those chores, but he did pick apples and berries and now and then he cooked, superbly. (His much-discussed rolled flank steak stuffed with anchovy butter and some shallots never did come off, though, because we could never assemble all of the ingredients from our island markets.) His habits are nocturnal, quite opposite to ours. He would rise late, about the time we would be concluding such writing as we regularly do. Breakfast barely broke the fast, consisting of a strong—never strong enough—cup of black coffee and furtive nibbles at a slice of bread.

Thereupon, he would prepare for his daily trek through the fields to the cliffs leading precariously to the sea. Preparation involved assembling some books, note paper and pen, some fruit, and a costume deemed suitable for the shore. In bad weather a slicker would be included. His choice of headgear—*hat* is definitely not the word—witnessed that even in the realm of the absurd a sort of discrimination is possible. Seldom would he ascend from the sea much before the sun sank into whatever is left of Long Island. He and I would share a few dollops of bourbon while Stringfellow, excused from that ceremony on account of health, made himself useful in the kitchen. Daniel eats sparsely but is tolerant of wine and just this side of gluttonous when the cheese arrives. But dinner was principally conversation, lamentations and rejoicings, wonderings and ponderings, and gratitudes for good men and women already in jail. Grace we sometimes uttered, but more often did not, on Stringfellow's contention that the meal had been amply blessed in the making of it.

After dinner Stringfellow, again on account of his health, would go, most often, to bed. Dan and I might talk on awhile but more likely, in deference to his total infatuation with the movies, we would watch on the idiot box some truncated classic of the silver screen. I recall once—before Block Island, before Catonsville, before bugged telephones and birdwatchers in the bushes—the three of us went one afternoon to see a film called, as I remember it (Shelley Winters was featured), *A Patch of Blue*. Stringfellow and I thought it was dreadful, but old Dan, munching his way through a box of stale popcorn, thoroughly enjoyed himself. (Later, in the months of his fugitive exile, he missed terribly going to the flicks, missed it so much, in fact, that several times he violated caution and went anyway. Thus he saw and greatly relished *Catch 22*, and in order, so he said, to investigate Richard Nixon's taste in cinema, *Patton*. Anyone, he decided, who would see *Patton* twice must have a thing about generals. I do not know what conclusion he drew from Mr. Nixon's celebrated exegesis of John Wayne's *Chisum*.) We would watch some film, Dan and I, and after the late news I would go to bed and he would go to work. I had the impression he usually worked deep into the night.

Such was the primitive liturgy of our days with Dan, scattered over several years, on Block Island.

Death, meanwhile, busybodied all about us and even *in* us, clouding even the most halcyon of our respite island days. The power of death was, as all the world knows, rampant in those years in the jungles and villages of Vietnam and in the streets, the ghettos, the plundered land of America. In Vietnam babies burned to death or worse in hamlets incinerated, some said, for their own salvation, and in America babies drank of death in their mothers' milk or died sometimes for lack of mothers' milk. So it goes, Kurt Vonnegut has said. Daniel Berrigan, a patient man, has, as a Christian, no patience with stoicism in the face of death. He raged and raged against the dying of the light. So, with his also outraged brother Philip and seven other intrepid Catholics, he burned with napalm some draft records, instruments of death, in Catonsville. Patiently the felons contemplated their crime and prayed, awaiting the wrath of injured authority. There would be an ordeal of justice, a trial.

William Stringfellow became more proximately a target of death's lambent aggressions. Painstaking and most efficient —like agents in an FBI crime laboratory—death picked and poked its way through that complex of organs known to us as Stringfellow. The pancreas proved vulnerable. Jubilant as a birdwatcher might be on sighting a prothonotary warbler, death took up residence in Stringfellow's pancreas and quickly established hegemony as well over the adjacent spleen. Pain ensued and drastic loss of weight. Specialists were beguiled. Medicines and therapies availed not. Hospitals profitably failed to remedy. There would be an ordeal of medicine, a surgery.

Both events, the trial and the surgery, were appointed, by chance or by providence, for the month of November of 1968.

An invitation as though to a wedding arrived from Daniel. Would we be sò kind as to attend his trial? Would we invite our good friend Bishop Pike? We would. When the week of the trial was upon us, early in November, it needed no doctor to say Stringfellow should not go. Anthony would go and there join Jim Pike. The trial is history and a book and now a play, art imitating life. On the evening of the third day of the trial, what remained of William Stringfellow did, in fact, appear. There were speeches being made to several thousands gathered in a Baltimore church. Stringfellow would utter (whisper) a few words, the last of them an admonition to remember that death has no dominion over us. Daniel Berrigan would say that William Stringfellow's life had been on the line for a very long time.

The Catonsville Nine, the jury concluded, were guilty, were criminals. They would, the judge decreed, go to jail for various numbers of years. But first there would be appeals. Daniel, now a criminal and felon for peace, not yet a fugitive for peace, would be free on bail. It would require, as things worked out, seventeen months for the appeals to grind their way to certain denial. The Berrigans and their friends, more and more friends, would not be idle those long months. Their war against the war would go on.

On the morning of November 22 of 1968, the fifth anniversary of the lethal ballistic surgery of John Kennedy, William Stringfellow went, as the tabloids describe it, under the knife. The evening preceding, Stuart Wetmore, an Episcopal bishop of New York and an old friend, would be gracious enough to preside over what amounted to an Anglican equivalent of the last rites. There would be a few closest friends. Dan Berrigan, by special permission of the court, would, of course, be among them. He would, of course, share with us the body and blood of Christ, tainted though some might suppose them to be by Henry VIII's petulant distemper some centuries earlier. No one present except William String-fellow expected William Stringfellow would survive the morrow's knife. He would, in fact, be under that knife more than ten hours. He would almost die. But between almost dying and dying yawns, for the living, the widest of gulfs.

The surgery would succeed. Stringfellow would live. He would be diabetic. He would suffer medications and restrictions and a precarious health. But he would live. He would even, after long convalescence, work. So, the day after the surgery Bishop Pike would come with Diane, soon to be his wife and then his widow. And Dan would come with a page of photographs taken at the Catonsville trial. These would hang on the wall of Stringfellow's room next to a circus poster sent by Sister Corita. Shortly they would be joined by obituaries of two other friends who were to die, Karl Barth and Thomas Merton. Stringfellow would live, but death had had nonetheless a plush harvest in the fall of 1968.

Students of history may wish to be reminded that it was also in November of 1968 that Richard Nixon was elected President of the United States.

There followed on Block Island, a long, bleak, and recuperative winter. Now and then Dan would call from his quarters at Cornell to ask after Bill. We would hear or see or read of the ongoing war against the war. Draft records had been burned first here, then there, and then, it seemed, all over the place. But the war, too, went on and on and on. I had been asked to do a book about deserters and draft exiles and war resisters, and in March of 1969 I went for some weeks to Stockholm. I met many young men, sons in the main of the Silent Majority, expelled like some rotten apple from Spiro Agnew's wholesome barrel of warriors. They did not choose to fight or die in a barbarous war in which they could not believe. That choice is a crime in America. I returned from Sweden depressed.

That summer Dan came for a lengthy stay on the island. We all assumed, I think, it would be his last before going to jail.

The Feast of the Assumption fell during his visit and upon learning that it would also be Dan's thirtieth anniversary of becoming a Jesuit, Father Kirkman, the priest of St. Andrew's on the island, invited him to celebrate the mass and to preach. The night before I had been telling Dan that the dogma of the Assumption was for me, as an Episcopalian, the most difficult to accommodate, more difficult even than the one about the infallibility of the Pope. I could conceive of a way of understanding infallibility which would allow assent. I had more of a problem with the bodily assumption of Mary. This had to do with the fact that whereas some other of the fustier dogmas are relics of centuries long gone and so can be cherished as one might cherish grandfather's clock (even though it keeps time poorly), the dogma of the Assumption has been only lately promulgated by Pius XII and so has to be coped with as one might cope with, say, an electric toothbrush, i.e., awkwardly. In an era when men are bodily assumed to the moon, Mary's bodily assumption into Heaven seemed to me not less but more incredible.

Dan did celebrate at St. Andrew's, elegantly, and he did preach in his quiet, insistent way. He spoke to my problem, deftly shifting the burden from my poor intellect to Mary, where, perhaps, it belongs; and he spoke of peace, especially of Mary's unique office as advocate for all of us whose prayers are prayers for peace. I remained unreconciled with the dogma of the Assumption, but found myself nearer to Mary than I had ever before felt myself to be. That may be what the dogma really means.

During that same, penultimate visit—almost precisely one year prior to his apprehension—Dan raised with us the query whether, when all appeals had duly exhausted themselves and a date fixed for going to jail, he and his brother and the others of the Catonsville Nine should, in fact, render themselves to Caesar. For Dan the issue did not have to do with the conventional ethics of the situation. His exclusive concern was how he and the others could most effectively perpetuate their witness against the war, their ministry for peace. He was not persuaded that the sole option was to conform with orthodox civil disobedience strategy: having made one's point one goes meekly off to prison to take the consequences. How, Dan wondered, would that hasten an end to the war? It might, on the contrary, by acceding to the authority of the State, embellish that State's authority to prolong the war. It might, in other words, render to Caesar authority properly reserved to God.

If a priest does not belong to God, who or what—in the name of the separation of State and Church—does? It is I who ask that question. Dan did not.

So, there was speculation about venerable issues. Perhaps some of the Nine should surrender, paying conventional respects to classic civil disobedience doctrine, but others should not, thereby asserting that it is God and not Caesar, imminently as well as finally, who has claim upon us all. The speculation became jocular and we all wondered whether, as between the brothers, one was more suited for prison than the other. Philip has a personality which, it was affirmed, would give him a relevant ministry among inmates, while Dan seemed more fit for a continuing articulate witness against the war enterprise through the assorted media technology has visited upon men. I may have been influenced, in these wonderings, by the happenstance that, like Dan, I am a poet. It is my considered opinion that any society that locks up priests is sick, and any society that imprisons poets is doomed.

The conversation became more animated when Stringfellow and I conceived another alternative. Perhaps Dan should not render himself to Caesar but instead render himself to the Pope. Why should he not, we fancied, betake himself to Rome to beseech of Paul sanctuary as a political refugee? Another celebrated priest who had experienced difficulties with secular authority—Thomas à Becket—had once received a similar asylum, it was recalled. Not only would that imaginatively prolong and enlarge the witness against the war, it would also pose to the Church of Christ, at its summit, a delicate and meet dilemma. Would the Vicar of Christ on Earth match with deed the eloquence of his many pronouncements against the war? Or would he return his prodigal son to secular authority and say, in effect, as the Archbishop of Baltimore had said generally of the Catonsville Nine, that he "washed his hands of the matter," thereby demonstrating, as Bishop Pike noted at the time, that "at least he reads his Scriptures"? We shall never, alas, know. Dan entertained our suggestion soberly, and thought he would discuss it with his brother. But what came of it we did not ever learn.

Somehow it seemed to me that Dan raised the whole question at that time speculatively more than intentionally. I did not have the impression that he really then contemplated not surrendering when the day came. And the concept of being a fugitive for peace as he was later to elaborate it did not emerge at all in those discussions. He had in mind, I think, more the idea of going into exile, after the manner of Eldridge Cleaver and many another black exile. We spoke, I recall, of the possibility of developing some kind of ministry among the deserters in Sweden or the war resistance community in Canada.

In one of our last conversations, a day or so before the birdwatchers interrupted, Dan was to speak of Eldridge Cleaver and his exile in Algeria. Cleaver must be, he contemplated, awfully lonely, more lonely than he would be in jail. Daniel Berrigan is one of those rare persons who seem always to be on the scene, where the action is. It may be simply that the scene, the action, is where such persons are. Whichever way it be, the scene, in my opinion, has now gone to jail, and Dan, I predict, will not be lonely there.

During the two weeks of that 1969 visit, Dan had spent much time at the island beaches and on the rocks at the foot of our cliffs, and when the day came to leave he was rested, tanned, and in high good spirits.

We remembered with joy the last time he had left the island, several months earlier. On that occasion, I had driven him to the island airport, where we waited some time for the small plane that would convey him to Providence. When, finally, it did land, out stepped none less than John Chaffee, then Governor of Rhode Island, arriving to do a bit of election-year fence-mending. (He mended too little or too late, the people rejected him and he lost the election, whereupon, after the curious fashion of American politics, President Nixon promptly elevated him to even greater responsibility as Secretary of the Navy.) Mr. Chaffee waved at—not *to*—us and forced up that ferocious grin candidates for public office inflict upon their potential subjects. Dan and I joked, as we returned his wave and something of his grin, how very appropriate it was that Caesar should render unto a felon for peace the temporary seat of his authority. Dan took that seat with splendid mock solemnity, flashed to—not *at*—me the peace sign, and was gone.

Stringfellow and I did not expect to see Dan again after the visit of the summer of 1969 until such time as we might visit him in prison. Indications were that appeals would soon be done with and that jail would ensue that fall. It turned out, however, that matters dragged through the winter and the time for jailing did not arrive until the following April.

As he has done in other years William Stringfellow accepted an invitation to preach in the chapel at Cornell in October of 1969. So, he would see Dan again. The weekend of his engagement chanced to coincide with a meeting of Cornell's trustees, called to consider the unrest rampant on that campus. The trustees would also decide what should be done about the controversial Catholic chaplain of Cornell, Daniel Berrigan. Before a congregation of students, faculty, and trustees, then, Stringfellow would preach and Father Berrigan would preside as liturgist.

The sermon was provocatively titled "Jesus as a Criminal." Its thesis was that Jesus was, in fact, guilty of the crimes against the state with which he was charged. No mention was made specifically of the situation of Daniel Berrigan, but the parallelisms were unescapable. The students were delighted, the faculty bemused, the trustees, for the most part, enraged. The wife of one trustee would sail back after the service and enthrall the preacher and the liturgist with a remarkable display of unladylike invective.

The trustees in their wisdom—and aware, no doubt, that to do otherwise would further inflame student discontent— elected to retain Father Berrigan, to grant him leave to serve his term in prison, and to permit his return once the state concluded his punishment was sufficient. Whether that decision will survive Father Berrigan's more recent criminal capers is, I would think, a moot question.

Jesus may have been a criminal but at least he had the civic decency not to become a fugitive.

Other than one or two brief telephone chats we heard no more from or of Dan that winter until early in April our radio informed us that he, his brother, and some others of the Catonsville Nine had failed to surrender to the authorities

and had become fugitives. We were not, as I have said, astonished, though we had had no prior information about it. It was
consistent with the conversation we had had with Dan the previous summer, and it was consistent with the adamant witness
against the war he and his brother had sustained for so long.

The vanishment of the Berrigans seemed to me a natural
metamorphosis of the strategy they had devised out of the
circumstances with which they were confronted. From priests
(or Christians) for peace they had become felons (or criminals)
for peace, and now they would become fugitives for peace and
—it was inevitable—sooner or later they would be prisoners
for peace. Their witness against the war would be as stubborn
as the war itself. No one who knew the Berrigans could harbor
doubt about that.

We were not surprised but we were, of course, concerned,
and so we wrote to Jerry Berrigan—another of that remarkable
set of brothers—to express our concern, and upon learning
that he held power of attorney for Dan and Phil and responsibility for the family's tattered finances, we sent what little
money we could for use at his discretion. Stringfellow tele-
phoned another of the chaplains at Cornell, who reported that
the following weekend there would be a mammoth festival at
Cornell—called "America Is Hard to Find"—and rumor had
it that Daniel Berrigan would "surface" at some point in those
proceedings. We were invited to participate, but other obliga-
tions denied us that pleasure.

Dan did—as was widely reported at the time—manifest himself during the Cornell festivities. "Surface" is the word used,
and in the months ahead that word was to be emphatically
added to the lexicon of the peace movement. He spoke before
some 10,000 young people and an unknown number of FBI
birdwatchers. He told the throng he would surrender if they
wanted him to. There was a deafening chorus of negatives.
Minutes later, having slipped into a masquerade figure of one

of the twelve apostles, he vanished again, leaving behind, the United States Attorney in Maryland later confessed, a lot of FBI agents with "egg on their faces." Philip Berrigan, meanwhile, had been captured at the church of St. Gregory in Manhattan, together with David Eberhardt, another of the Catonsville Nine. The two had planned to "surface" that same evening in a service at the church. FBI agents, having poked their way methodically through the rectory, smashed down a locked door to a study and found them in a closet.

Some days later our mail yielded the first in a series of "Notes from the Underground," a mimeographed report from fugitive Dan to the world at large. And we began to read in the church and secular press a stream of articles, comments, and interviews elucidating the estate of fugitive priests. Notably, we read in *Saturday Review* Dan's brilliant review, in the form of a prose poem, of Bethge's new life of Bonhoeffer. That prose poem I consider of itself is ample warrant for Daniel Berrigan's fugitive career. He must have written incessantly during those months of peripatetic exile, and he has never written more beautifully. Not a few writers through history have done exalted work while on the lam from some presumptive authority or other and gone on to do their most inspired work in prison. That is something with which those writers still out of jail may console themselves. There is, God knows, little else of consolation to be found in the darkness descending all about us.

We waited, Stringfellow and I, knowing that in the fullness of time more direct word would come. One day there came a note, bubbling with that sense of fun Dan brings to any of his endeavors, and composed in what I can only call a mock-cryptic style. It *might* have confused an agent of the FBI or some other auditor or censor—but I doubt it—and no reader of the writings of Daniel Berrigan could have failed to identify its author. He would, we deciphered, welcome an opportunity

to talk with old friends in the next week or two. Would a
setting somewhere in the neighborhood of Boston be convenient? It seemed as good a spot as any for so bizarre a
rendezvous.

Further mock-cryptic notes were exchanged. Alas, the notes
were all discarded. It is a pity. Published as parodies of clandestine communications they might have garnered some presti-
gious prize. On a certain date we would go to Logan Airport
in Boston. On the mezzanine of a terminal there we would
find a shop operated by S. S. Pierce. We would purchase a bar
of dietetic chocolate. *Somebody* would notice that, present
themselves, and give us directions.

The appointed date arrived, but with it arrived also dense
fog, and air connections between Block Island and America
were suspended. The rendezvous could not be kept. God,
William Stringfellow said, obviously doesn't want us to meet
Dan today.

We had plans for a journey in mid-June to Geneva, New
York. We would attend there the graduation from Hobart
College of Rafael Martinez, good friend whom we had sponsored into higher education. It would be a leisurely trip of
about a week by rented car. We would also visit Stringfellow's
parents in Northampton, Massachusetts, and Anthony's sister
in Middlebury, Vermont. We would accept an invitation for
dinner from Jerry and Carol Berrigan in Syracuse, New York.
Perhaps God willed that we add our rendezvous with Dan
onto that journey.

Another exchange of mock-cryptic notes ensued. Yes, that
could be done, and a new date for rendezvous was set. *That*
date arrived and with it some friends on a motor trip through
New England. They would be delighted to drive us to Boston
and drop us at Logan Airport. Marmaduke, the only Christian
dog, would also make the journey. A dietetic chocolate bar
was purchased in the mezzanine shop operated by S. S. Pierce.

A woman admired Marmaduke. (She may have been a former nun. There is something *about* former nuns. But I won't go into that lest I wander too far afield.) We would rent a car, have supper, and drive to an address in suburban Boston.

The neighborhood and the house to which we went were elegant and elm-endowed. Daniel Berrigan looked very well and had gained weight. Marmaduke was very happy to see him. A bottle of excellent bourbon appeared and a pot of very strong black coffee. *This* underground, I remarked, is a fairly comfortable way of life. Dan did not deny it—he loved it, I think —but he did confess that it was exhausting. Fugitives are human, he said, and like everybody else need an occasional vacation. He yearned for some days at the foot of our cliffs. Marmaduke would be honored if he would come for a visit. The risks were not discussed. Intelligent people do not have to discuss what they already know. He wanted to come. He would.

We had talked less than an hour. We would all have liked to talk all night. But the weather was an outrage of heat. William Stringfellow was wilting visibly, Marmaduke was hungry, and Anthony was nervous. He had never expected to be "underground" even for less than an hour. We departed in search of a motel with an air-conditioned vacancy. Anthony, for the first time in his life, studied the rear-view mirror. He did not know what to look for. But so far as he could tell no birdwatchers were in his wake.

We found in due course a motel that would do, fed the dog, and went to bed to sleep a fitful sleep. Next morning we continued on to Northampton for lunch with Stringfellow's parents, and left Marmaduke with them. That evening we flew to Syracuse for our dinner engagement with Jerry and Carol Berrigan.

They also serve who only stand and wait. Besides raising four small children and both working, it had become Jerry and Carol's job to attend to personal affairs for the felonious twosome and to care for the aged mother of all the Berrigans, lately widowed. We delivered them an envelope Dan had given us which he said contained papers Jerry should keep for him. Mother Berrigan, we learned, had recently broken her hip. During her surgery armed agents of the FBI stood vigil lest her fugitive son be so imprudent as to pay her a call in this extremity. Berrigans are sometimes imprudent, as the world measures such things, but they are never stupid and they have Irish fortitude galore. Daniel did not visit his mother nor did she expect him to. She would endure her lot as he endured his. And happily she would survive it.

Jerry and Carol had also been paying regular visits to Philip at the federal penitentiary in Lewisburg. Each visit they would take with them two of the children in order that they should never forget to be proud of their uncle. Philip, they reported, was being held in maximum security (solitary confinement) as apparent hostage for the fugitive Daniel. Phil's spirits were low and his rage against authority escalating daily. Only one thing would likely enrage him more. That would be for brother Dan to surrender in an effort to persuade authority to mitigate his punishment. Fat chance, we all agreed, of that.

Carol served us a meal which, in fact, was that rarity, a feast. The salad dressing, I recall, was made from her father's own wine. From such ingredients and the love of life, feasts are born. All about us were mementos of Dan. Upon his sudden disappearance, Carol had inherited for the unforeseeable future the vivid embellishments that had made of his rooms and office at Cornell an enchantment for myriad students.

Works of Corita Kent livened the walls. [Dear Corita: you will always be *Sister* to many of us.] Her brash exuberance—half circus, half *Madison* Avenue and all Resurrection—assured us that no gloom would invade our dinner conversation.

None did. But even joyous chatter is strained when J. Edgar

Hoover is overhearing it. Outside the Berrigan home has been for months a bevy of birdwatchers. Inside, even the dining room was bugged. Legally? Illegally? Who can say? Who can prevent J. Edgar from overhearing any dinner conversation he chooses to overhear? Richard Nixon? *Ha!* John Mitchell? Double *ha!* Any people that elevates and enshrines snoops debases itself. One learns, alas, to live with it. I have lately resigned myself to the grisly fact that even my middle-of-the-night mutterings are relentlessly being recorded and stored away in the belly of some gross computer.

So, we talked of cabbages and kings—and many things. (For a full transcript, apply to J. Edgar Hoover, Washington, D.C.) We talked, I remember, at length about what *finally* was the meaning of the splendid witness of Daniel and Philip. William Stringfellow put it well, I thought, when he said that they had been telling us, showing us what it means to be human.

Another night in another motel, sleep less fitful on account of the solidarity of faith and love, and next morning we proceeded to Geneva, New York, for the commencement at Hobart College and exposure to yet another dimension of the national dementia. It was specifically for the graduation of Rafael Martinez that we had come. But there would be also old friends to stay with and new friends to make. It would be, if not a feast, a festival.

Rafael we had known many a year from many a long-ago battle in Harlem and the politics of urban jungles. He lacked a college education, having had to support a mother and innumerable sisters. It was a lack we thought required repair. We had, and have, in mind that with a decent gringo education he would make one day a fine first president of an independent Puerto Rico. So, with much help from many quarters, we had sponsored a higher education for Rafael, now, astonishingly, about to conclude with his graduation from Hobart at age 37. I found it hard to think of the event as a commencement. One does not commence at age 37.

During his years at Hobart, Rafael had often seen Dan Berrigan. Cornell is not so far away and Dan had, in effect, functioned as a sort of surrogate father for us at times when that role had to be played by somebody. There had been visits back and forth. Rafael had been sometimes to dinner at Dan's, relishing, I suppose, rolled flank steak with anchovy butter stuffing. Notice how everything fits together. You have what is called by silent majoritarians and birdwatchers a *conspiracy*. Normal living, I submit, if there is any love in it, is one long, gorgeous and, no doubt, subversive conspiracy, subversive, anyhow, of such other conspiracies as the Silent Majority and the FBI. I plead myself guilty here and now of standing in conspiracy with anybody who is bored to tears with the Silent Majority and revolted by the FBI, the CIA, and all other domestic or foreign, clandestine gestapos.

Coffee was had with Rafael. There had been a few disquieting events. He had been involved, in this last academic year as he had been all along, in a variety of student and community protests and actions. In these connections he had met one "Tommy the Traveler," a heavy in the Hobart undergraduate radical and drug scene, though not a student of that college. He had come to have reason to suspect that Tommy the Traveler was, in fact, a plant, an informer for law enforcement agencies. He disclosed his suspicions to the school administrators and others. Disbelief and even scorn greeted his disclosures. Rafael, some suggested, had contracted a mild paranoia. His paranoia did not diminish when he heard that Tommy the Traveler had made threats against his life.

Tommy was known as the Traveler because he professed to move from campus to campus in pursuit of revolutionary action. He was, apparently, a ready source of drugs and even of dynamite. His skills included the making of explosives, a talent he was eager to share with his fellow revolutionaries. He had achieved on the Hobart compus some status as a hero of the radical left.

Toward the end of the school year the ROTC building was burned. Some students were shortly charged with the crime. Rafael had been picked up by the police. Where was Daniel Berrigan? (He did not know.) Why had he gone in 1951—at age 18—to Cuba? (He had visited pre-Castro Cuba because his father took him there on a vacation.) Why had he spent 1968–1969 in Mexico? (He had done his third academic year as a transfer student at the University of Mexico.) Why had he gone for two weeks from Mexico to Guatemala? (A girl friend had invited him to spend the school vacation with her family.) Rafael was released. He had had nothing whatever to do with the burning of the ROTC building.

There was a brief hiatus and then one night two police cars —one containing Tommy the Traveler—arrived on the Hobart campus. Led by Tommy, a student room was raided, narcotics were alleged to have been found, some students were arrested and taken off to jail. The police cars returned. Enraged students surrounded them, used ungracious language, severed radio antennas, and otherwise discommoded the occupants, including Tommy the Traveler.

It was a crisis. The college president was alarmed. He asked that Rafael Martinez be located. No one else, he thought, could prevail on the students to desist from violence. Rafael was found in a downtown bar drinking beer with friends. He returned at once to the campus. He helped mediate an agreement. The police would release and drop charges against the students and the students would release without further discomfort the police. The mediation succeeded. There would be no riot that night.

Two days later Rafael and several other students were summarily arrested and charged with offenses related to the campus disturbance. Before being booked they were forcibly shaved and given slovenly haircuts. (Rafael had had a magnificent beard, most fastidiously groomed.) After a comedy of absurdity a bail was set and paid and the shorn prisoners were freed. Adam Walinsky, a candidate for attorney general of New York State, intervened in these proceedings, professing outrage. Governor Nelson Rockefeller acquired a concern, supervened all lesser authorities, caused to be impaneled a special grand jury, and said its conclusions would have his personal attention.

Tommy the Traveler was indeed a paid informer, a plant, so it turned out, of the county sheriff having jurisdiction in that place. A man, from my cursory observation, endowed by nature with few visible gifts, that sheriff allowed it to be known that Tommy had come into his employ recommended by higher authority, unidentified. Might that higher authority have been the FBI, our friends the birdwatchers? We must pray not. What a state of affairs it would be if the FBI routinely should plant men on campuses to encourage use of drugs and bombs in order to create situations that would permit the arrest of misguided students. Surely the FBI does not share the good sheriff's opinion, publicly stated, that Tommy the Traveler did no wrong in teaching students to make bombs so long as he did not teach them how to use the bombs.

Our coffee with Rafael had grown cold. I had resorted to a brandy. But the immediate outcome, anyhow, was some relief. The Hobart faculty had voted that Rafael would be awarded his degree despite the inconvenient fact that he had flunked chemistry. We had not made our long journey to no avail. There would later on be a cocktail party. Life would go on. Anthony would take a nap.

That evening William Stringfellow would deliver for some students the anticommencement address, a custom of the place in recent years. Daniel Berrigan had been the anticommencement speaker one year previous. Stringfellow was to discern in the now situation of America parallels to the terminal situation of Babylon as recorded in the Book of Revelation. He was also to discern some parallels to the situation of Germany in the 1930's. His remarks had been prepared before reaching Hobart, but the saga of Rafael Martinez and Tommy the Traveler cannot but have strengthened the conviction of his delivery. College education, I remember reflecting, had certainly changed in remarkable ways in the two-odd decades since I had suffered my way through it.

Graduation day dawned bright and clear and rapidly became an atrocity of heat. Rafael appeared toward the end of the morning fresh from what I took to have been an all-night wing-ding. His disaffection from the establishment had reached such a point, said he, that it would not be possible for him to march in *their* commencement procession. Anthony announced that he had not come several hundred precarious miles to hear William Stringfellow herald the end of the world. Rafael would march. He even would wear a cap and gown. But, it was to develop, this is *all* he would wear. Rafael marched buck naked under his cap and gown. I must say, given the heat of the day, I wish I had had the sense to attend the wretched event buck naked myself.

Nearby the ceremonies some hundreds of hard hats were allowed to march mouthing the buffoon banalities lately spewed across the land by Spiro Agnew and company. Above this parade of righteous indignation a sea of Old Glories proudly waved. But there was no violence. There was no confrontation. It was much too hot to confront anything. A black lady said to be from a high echelon of government labored her way through an eloquent commencement exposition, the substance of which eluded me entirely. She received a warm ovation. I had the feeling she was applauded because she was black and spoke nice English. The two are not supposed very often to coincide.

Degrees were awarded—endless degrees, one by one. Finally one could see that the name of Rafael Martinez would be

called. I observed the county sheriff frantically instructing his
photographer how to capture for his scrapbook the lion he
had a few days earlier bearded in a detention cell. That sheriff
was more delighted, I could tell, than most fathers are when
they witness the separation from the family payroll of its
principal drain. I cannot say that I was delighted in the same
way. There were, to be candid about it, tears in my eyes.
"Rafael Martinez!" By God, he got it! The students and many
of the faculty—but not, alas, the parents—rose and cheered.
It was enough. I felt the sort of emotion I wish I had felt
upon my own college graduation.

That was that. Next day Stringfellow and I proceeded to
Middlebury, Vermont, to spend a day with my sister in her
fine new woodland home. In that lovely and remote country it
was possible for an instant to imagine one did not live in a
society torn by its own irrationalities into shreds of self-destruc-
tion. And then we returned to Northampton to recover Marmaduke the Christian dog. We would also see Stringfellow's
old Aunt Polly. We would not see her again.

Daniel Berrigan could not come to Block Island until
William and Anthony and Marmaduke returned. This they
now did. It was, all three agreed, good to be home. Fred, the
Siamese cat, also known as the wretched ratcatcher, was glad
to see them all.

The grapevine fluttered. Another cryptic message drifted in
on a gentle breeze from interstellar space. Important assign-
ments had arisen. The fugitive would have to put off a vacation. Sometime in the month of August might do. We should
await a further word. So be it. Assorted relatives would be
shuttled in and out for their annual visitations. That would
take care of *them* and would spare them any danger of being
exposed to fugitive criminal priests. Between relatives, William
and Anthony would pursue their craft. They would do some
writing.

In mid-July there would come a letter from Sister Elizabeth, heretofore unknown to us. Some folks, she would say, have burned up some draft records in Wilmington, Delaware. Some other folks propose to make a statement accepting moral responsibility for that action together with the actual felons. Would William Stringfellow and Anthony Towne sign such a statement? They might, but first they would want to know more about it. Sister Elizabeth, they deduced, lived somewhere in the New York City area. William would shortly be in New York City. He would have breakfast with Sister Elizabeth.

He would be enchanted—Sister Elizabeth is a living doll. The statement would be publicly read in Wilmington, she said, and the signers and the proximate culprits would be there. Would Stringfellow consent to address the gathering? Would he undertake to place the action within a theological, a biblical framework? It would require fortitude I think, to say no to Sister Elizabeth. William Stringfellow said yes. The event would take place in the early part of August.

The grapevine fluttered wildly. Another cryptic message fairly hurtled in upon us. Daniel Berrigan would soon come to Block Island. William Stringfellow wrote to Sister Elizabeth. It did not appear, he regretted to say, that he would be able to speak in Wilmington.

On Monday, August 3, we were to read in the papers that Father Daniel Berrigan had surfaced the previous day in the First United Methodist Church of Germantown, Pennsylvania. He had preached for some twenty minutes and then he had vanished. That, we told each other, is quite some distance from Block Island.

Three days later, Thursday, August 6—anniversary of the dropping of the atomic bomb at Hiroshima and anniversary of the birth of Anthony's mother—there came a telephone call. A student with a manuscript wished to come and visit us. Might he come the following evening on the ferry with his wife and child? That, he was told, would be convenient. It must be that Daniel is coming to Block Island, said Anthony. Perhaps, said William, it is a student with a manuscript and a wife and a child. We would have to wait and see.

Next morning we drove to the island airport to pick up some medicine for Stringfellow. A man stepped from an airplane and entered a waiting car. As we started to drive out of the airport the man emerged from the car and hailed us. He was, he said, a Jesuit priest and he gave us his name. His hostess on the island had told him we were friends of Father Berrigan. We confessed our guilt. We had not, he hazarded, heard from Daniel Berrigan lately. We allowed his observation to stand on its merits. Perhaps, Anthony said, while he was on the island he would come by for a drink. He would first get settled and then he would call.

Anthony met the Friday evening ferry, which was mobbed and arrived after the sun had set. He stood near the end of the pier and peered. He did not see Daniel Berrigan. He drove back to the house. There had come a telephone call. The student could be found across from the church at the entrance to Spring Street. We drove to that location. There we found a student, a wife, a child—and Daniel Berrigan. We did not find any manuscript. Dan looked tired. He had shaved his whiskers. He was very cheerful.

In the circumstances, what could follow other than a feast?

It was a merry feast. But the hour grew late. The guest room would be assigned to the student, the wife, the child—and the mythical manuscript. Where to sleep Dan? Anthony's study would do nicely. Indeed, why should not Dan just take over Anthony's study for the duration? That study had been created from what had been a small stable to the rear of the house. In it Anthony's *Excerpts from the Diaries of the Late God* had been completed. For these reasons, a friend had named the place "the manger." Daniel Berrigan would sleep and work in the manger. A foldaway bed was trundled out and that was that. A few days later a Providence paper was to headline a front-page story: HE HID IN THE MANGER. Well, he didn't *hide* there. He worked there and he slept there.

Aunt Polly had died. Tomorrow would be her funeral. Anthony would rise very early and drive William to the airport. A plane had been arranged to fly him to Northampton for the service. He would return the same way in time for dinner. Anthony returned to the house and began to make breakfasts, first for this one, then for that one and finally, toward noon, he made a pot of insufficiently strong coffee for Daniel Berrigan. The student, the wife, and so forth were driven to catch the early afternoon ferry. At last, said Dan, he could descend the cliffs to the sea. He vested for the occasion. He would not be seen again until time for predinner bourbon.

It had been solacing and solitary by the sea. Other than two youngsters who passed by he had seen no one. That is not surprising. Our shoreline is remote, rocky, and hard to get to. Later there would be a rumor on the island that Daniel Berrigan had been recognized on the beach by some children. But there were to be many rumors. Another had it that he was seen in broad daylight in the middle of the village. That was certainly not the case. We do not know how or by whom the FBI learned that Daniel Berrigan was on Block Island. Maybe he *was* recognized by some children on our beach. Maybe, unbeknownest to us, our house had been under some kind of continuous surveillance throughout Dan's fugitive career. Maybe, though I doubt it, someone had recognized him during the ferry trip. Or maybe—there had been just prior to his coming to the island several close calls—an informer from some other place had rendered to Caesar a tip. And, of course, it is possible there was some combination of such misfortunes.

No one on Block Island—other than William and Anthony —knew Dan Berrigan was coming and no one on the island knew he was there until his presence became conspicuous by reason of his capture. Though we had assumed some island people would drop by during his visit none did. On the Monday of his stay the young lady who regularly cleaned the house came as usual, but Dan was on the beach and she did not, I am confident, see him. There are houses near enough to us for the inhabitants to have noticed that we had a guest, but none is near enough for them to have been able to identify that guest. Someone studying the property with field glasses could have done so, but the only person likely to be that curious would be a government birdwatcher.

The FBI (Federal Birdwatchers Inc.?), for whatever its words may be worth, has publicly stated that it did not know how long Daniel Berrigan had been on Block Island and that the information of his being there had come from the island.

The matter of paranoia merits mention. One of the unseemly consequences of a repressive (or polarized) society is that citizens ordinarily of balanced mind develop paranoid tendencies. Evidence for this is, I submit, presently provided for this society by a cursory examination of most any daily paper. But I am competent to testify about it only from my own experience, and I do so with the *caveat* that, as a poet, I have always been paranoid and my experiences of late have, I concede, merely magnified a condition that already existed. My enduring suspicion that reality is not what it is made out to be has suffered grotesque exacerbation.

Daniel Berrigan, during his fugitive poethood, wrote for *The Village Voice* an illuminating and odd piece about fear. In it he commented upon the fear he had seen in the faces of friends and hosts compelled by conscience and love to place themselves in a jeopardy they would normally have eschewed. That fear, of course, was in one sense natural—fear is an appropriate response to a situation of danger—but in another sense it is not natural to have fear when one acts in love and good conscience. For those of us who are Christians, especially, our faith in the Resurrection ought to still fear in us when we act in love.

It is not, I regret to say, my experience that faith drives out fear in times of extraordinary pressure. On the contrary, fear takes possession of one, transforming elements of sensible apprehension into instruments of unholy terror. It is upon such unholy terror, I suspect, that governments of repression depend. I became during the period attendant to Daniel Berrigan's sojourn on Block Island possessed of suspicions of our friends, our neighbors, and the world in general. I saw what was not there and I subjected myself to nightmares while actually wide awake.

Before there *were* birdwatchers in the bushes I sensed their furtive, restless agitations, and in each vehicle that passed the property I discerned hostile passengers, even when I knew the vehicle and its occupants to be friends.

One of those friends, of course, may have been no friend at all!

Into my mind at the time returned the refrain of a poem I had not read or thought of in perhaps twenty years. It was a poem from earliest English and I recall nothing of it now but the refrain, which was in Latin: *Timor mortis conturbat me.* That refrain haunted me during Dan's visit and ever since, much as one is sometimes taken over by the jingle from a radio commercial or by the trite lyric of some song that recalls a long-dead adolescent love affair. *Timor mortis conturbat me!* Indeed it does. Death has, in fact, *conturbate*d me from the time I first became aware that I had the fortune to be alive.

But why should death have put me into so great conturbation at precisely a moment when I knew myself to be living for once beyond the reach of death? I was living in the Resurrection and I knew it. Literally, I had no doubt. Why, then, should I be captive of so much fear? Precedents from the Scriptures are numerous. It is inaccurate, I think, to speak of *doubting*

Thomas. Thomas did not doubt. He feared. He should be called *fearing* Thomas. He feared that the absence of doubt in him might mark him special prey of death. He feigned doubt on account of this fear. Feigned doubt is paranoia. Why did Anthony fear when he had nothing *to* fear? Assuming the posture of undoubting Thomas Aquinas, *I answer:* Anthony was afraid not to be afraid.

How ludicrous his afraidness made him! To fear a birdwatcher is, on the face of it, absurd. To fear a fake birdwatcher plumbs the depths of humiliation. Just the other day a real birdwatcher came to the door. She was, she said, desolate because in two days of intensive search she had found not one cuckoo. Anthony forebore to tell her that her quest was at an end.

Paranoia is a social disease. It is highly communicable, tending toward epidemic fertility. Our most immediate island neighbors swiftly succumbed. On the Monday preceding Tuesday's apprehension, most of them endured visitations from birdwatchers. One such family has reported that a personage invaded their home in the absence of the paterfamilias and announced that he was in hot pursuit of a fugitive. He declined to identify the fugitive (though he did identify himself), nor would he indicate the dreadful crime for which his quarry was sought. The lady of the household, in process of preparing fish for her brood's supper, not surprisingly envisaged a sex maniac on the loose. She did her best to be helpful. Fortunately, that lady is possessed of a loose and ample humanity and is not the sort fake birdwatchers are disposed to trust. They withdrew from her household, leaving her in a state of some terror. She summoned the local constabulary. It had no knowledge of the matter. Despite its professed concern for local law enforcement, the incumbent zealots of law and order neglected to advise local or state police of their birdwatching adventure.

Another neighbor couple of silent majority persuasion wel-

comed the birdwatchers onto their property without having
been told who was sought—or why. They did so, the unliber-
ated female spouse declared, because the FBI can go anywhere
it wants to. She unquestionably believes that. By such defaults
decent men and women seduce tyrants. On account of such
defaults the FBI *does,* in fact, go anywhere it wants to. That
is why they have been suffered to listen in upon (unrepri-
manded) the personal telephone conversations of the late
Martin Luther King, Jr. That is why by act of Congress—the
Constitution notwithstanding—the FBI will shortly roam at
random our nation's campuses, and by another act of Congress
will occupy our international and many of our domestic airplane flights. Bit by ever larger morsel, America surrenders
its freedom to vultures in birdwatchers' clothing.

Paranoia, however, did not afflict Daniel Berrigan's roughly
four days on Block Island, because he was himself so radiantly
free of it. He knew the birdwatchers might be in the bushes.
He knew they might not be in the bushes. He was content to
wait. From some bush some day a birdwatcher *would* emerge.
On that day Dan would greet him as one would greet an old
friend who had become somehow a competitor but was no
less for that a companion in life's grim comedy. Between the
criminal and the cop, between the prisoner and the jailer,
between the bird and the birdwatcher, there is a comity not
lightly to be distinguished from love. Dan did not fear the
birdwatchers. He awaited them with a special tenderness,
lovingly. They had been for some time most solicitous of him;
he would be no less solicitous of them.

So, our conversation with Dan proceeded. How long it might
have lasted I do not know. My guess would be that it might
have gone on for ten days or two weeks. That would have
sufficed for a proper fugitive vacation and would also, I
venture, have exhausted the elaborate, many-leveled discussion
in which we were so desultorily engaged. But the fact is that we

never considered how long he would remain and we had no plan whatever about when or how he would make a departure. Anthony had declared that, having given up his study to Dan, he would himself be on vacation for the duration of the visit. He was, therefore, anxious that the visit be prolonged. It is Anthony's view that poets differ radically from other people, and prosper most under a regimen that consists of about two weeks work per annum and fifty weeks vacation.

One evening we talked about the movement Dan had been leading for so long in so many imaginative ways. What was needed now? That question was to come up repeatedly. On this occasion I remember stating bluntly that I thought the movement badly needed *depersonalization*. From the time of the Catonsville action the movement had depended too much upon the personalities of the Berrigans, and during the fugitive era it depended almost entirely on the personality of Daniel Berrigan. That personality happened to be charismatic enough to sustain the burden for quite some time, but obviously a time would come when it would not, and in the event Dan were captured the movement would risk decapitation, a very disordering experience. In retrospect, it seems to me the solitary flaw in Dan's brilliant underground performance is that public attention tended to focus upon the personal drama—Dan Berrigan versus the FBI—somewhat to the detriment of the message that drama was designed to convey.

Many people have wondered in the aftermath of the apprehension whether or not Dan came to Block Island *intending* to be captured. He would answer, I have no doubt, that he had done no such thing. I am not so sure. Certainly, nothing that he said while with us would suggest that he anticipated the event that terminated his visit. On the contrary, his talk was all of the future, of what might now be done, of possible surfacings, of actions that might broaden his witness, of moving to the Middle West and perhaps to the Far West. Least of all was he prepared to give up at a time when his brother was being held in solitary confinement as hostage against his witness.

Dan thought of his visit to the island, I have said, as a vacation, what Richard Nixon, I suppose, would call a *working* vacation. But there is not much distance, I think, between a vacation and a cessation. There were signs in his conversation that he despaired of being able to continue effectively. He was deeply offended that he had not had the support he believed warranted from the clergy of his own and other churches. He said several times by way of reproach to the Christian community that he had been *disproportionately* well received by Jews during his fugitive exile. He might have added a similar comment about nuns. But that was about it. Philip was in jail. *Why*, he would ask over and over again, *are there no bishops in jail?* That was the refrain which punctuated our several days of conversation. Dan was deeply distressed about the default of bishops.

It *is* a scandal for the church that there are no bishops in jail, as it is a scandal for the world that Philip (and now Daniel) *is* in jail. Daniel Berrigan was urgently preoccupied with both scandals. He was enraged that his brother should be in jail for loving peace too much and bishops should not be in jail for loving it too little. Woe be unto any bishop who squats comfortably his throne while those twin scandals persist.

William Stringfellow and Anthony Towne subscribe by mail to *The New York Times*. It comforts them. Its weight awes. Its amazing capacity for the digestion of information reassures. Daily an age of utter chaos is calmly, neatly ordered. Only the profusion of typographical errors betrays that the editors of the *Times* are, in fact, appalled at what they must record. Sunday's *Times* reaches Block Island on Monday. It is soon enough. By then fully two-thirds of it can safely be dispensed

with. That means one stands some chance of getting through
the balance by the weekend. There is virtually no news in the
Times. Most of it is ads, much of it consists of comment on
what *was* news several days before, and the rest speculates on
what *may* be news several days later. No news is good news.
The *Times* is a cornucopia of good news.

The Sunday *Times* of August 9 reached us Monday, August
10, and by nightfall—as the birdwatchers gathered in the
bushes—Daniel Berrigan had found two items of good news
in what is called "The News of the Week in Review." There
was a letter, signed by two prominent psychiatrists, protesting
the irregular, inhumane treatment being visited upon Philip
Berrigan (and David Eberhardt) in Lewisburg Penitentiary as
punishment for Daniel's fugitive intransigence. There was also
a feature story, with photograph, about Dan's startling epiphany one week earlier in the First Methodist Church of Germantown, Pennsylvania. Both items cheered Dan and were to
serve as fundaments of what proved to be our last evening of
conversation.

The birdwatchers were even then gathering in the bushes
though we did not know it. Our neighbors were having the
visitations I have described. Many on the island knew federal
agents were accumulating on the island. No one knew why.
It was widely assumed that the invasion had something to do
with a drug problem that had been distressing some of the
citizens. How many agents were involved in tracking down
the fugitive priest may never be known. We saw about a dozen
at the time of the apprehension. We know others were in
the immediate vicinity. Others were positioned strategically
throughout the island—at the airport, the ferry landings, even
the gas station. During those same days, agents interrogated
Robert Hoyt, editor of the *National Catholic Reporter,* whom
they mistook for Dan, in the airport at St. Louis; and in Los
Angeles, where Dan's play (based on the Catonsville trial) was

being presented, there were agents in the theater at each performance.

On that last evening, as the sun set, we had observed three rather large fishing vessels drop anchor in the harbor in a way that effectively blocked access to or egress from it. This was not a usual happening and we had joked that the CIA must be closing in. It was later stated that the vessels were, in fact, harmless Costa Rican fishing ships. I find that unreassuring, in that I have an impression Costa Rica may be a wholly owned subsidiary of the CIA. Be that as it may, it is incontestable that the birdwatchers had mounted a massive operation one might reasonably wish would be mounted to apprehend the many fugitives abroad in the land who constitute an authentic menace to society.

It must be recorded also that the same last evening came a telephone call from the Jesuit priest whose arrival on the island the same day Dan arrived has been mentioned. He would be leaving the island by plane, he said, the following afternoon. He would be amenable to stopping by for a drink just prior to that flight. He would, however, call again before doing so. Dan knew of the priest and had met him but did not know him well. It was nice, he remarked, to have a brother on the island and it would be nice to have him off it. The priest never called again. Some days later his hostess on the island told us the priest had left by ferry because the weather prevented any flying. He did not know of Dan's apprehension when he left, she said, and had asked her to call us expressing his regrets that the drink could not be had.

One must assume a rather remarkable coincidence in this matter, but my paranoia is such that I remain open to other and more sinister interpretations.

There was, then, a certain uneasiness that last evening, accentuated by the weather, which had taken a blustery turn portending, denizens of the island sensed, that the morrow would bring, if nothing else, a northeast storm. Stringfellow of the poor health retired early. Daniel and Anthony alternated discussion of the two items in the Sunday *Times* with perusal of a movie called *The Train,* having to do in a most complicated way with the French resistance in World War II. Dan was to wonder wistfully how a train might be used in the *American* resistance. Anthony, as has been said, was uneasy, but his uneasiness did not formulate itself into a conviction that birdwatchers were moving in. Daniel may or may not by then have entertained such a thought. Several times during the movie he would go abruptly from the house to the manger. It was Anthony's assumption that he did so to fetch one of the antacid tablets he used to quiet a dyspeptic stomach. But his distress may have had more ominous roots. He was not, however, to mention any suspicions he may have been suffering.

The letter to the *Times* about Philip and David Eberhardt obviously greatly comforted Dan. We both were convinced it would lead to early rectification of the conditions the two hapless hostages were enduring. Remedy was to come more swiftly than we expected, no doubt abetted by the taking of Dan the following morning. There is reason to believe that several United States senators (and at least two Princes of the Church) intervened at high levels of the administration. Shortly after Dan's capture and incarceration in Danbury Penitentiary Philip would be transferred from Lewisburg to Danbury, where the two brothers would be allowed to consort with one another and where they would be treated as decently as men are likely to be in indecent surroundings. As for David Eberhardt he would be taken out of solitary confinement in Lewisburg.

I remember remarking to Dan just before the evening concluded that one of the severe burdens of his fugitive estate was that he could not pick up the telephone and call members of his family and close friends to share with them his joy that effective measures were in the works to deliver Philip from the more intolerable dimensions of his agony.

We talked more extendedly that night about the other item in the *Times,* the feature story about the Germantown manifestation. It was a good story and Dan was pleased that the *Times* had given appropriate attention to what was, after all, a significant happening. What diminished his appreciation of the story, however, was a criticism of him for not having been specific enough about just what he would have those who agreed with him *do* about the war and the other issues he had dramatized. He was—I believe I choose the right word—*hurt* about that criticism, which seemed to reflect not only the view of the reporter but the views as well of others who had been interviewed in connection with the story.

He had, he noted, burned draft records. Wasn't that specific? He was currently a fugitive. Was that unspecific? His brother was in jail and in solitary confinement. How specific could you get? Daniel and Anthony, both poets, wasted little time over the story's suggestion that the alleged lack of specificity stemmed from Dan's poethood. Poets, they agreed, are the most specific people on earth. That is what poetry is all about. Perhaps Dan should write a poem, Anthony hazarded. No, Daniel decided, he would be specific like a journalist; that was clearly what was wanted. He would next day put together some specific suggestions for the unpoetic. Perhaps Anthony and William would help him. It might be they could assemble something collectively that could be transmitted to the *Times* to occupy the abhorred vacuum.

It would be idle to speculate about the details of a document events were to abort. But I can, I think, drawing upon the whole of our several days of conversation, indicate general areas upon which that document would surely have touched. It was no purpose of Daniel Berrigan, nor is it of William

Stringfellow and Anthony Towne, to tell others how to live their lives. That is a device more to the talents of Spiro Agnew. That Dan Berrigan is in jail should not be taken to mean that he has any wish to instruct any other man or woman to join him there. He is in jail primarily as a Christian. That is to say, Dan Berrigan has gone to jail for you and for me and for William Stringfellow. He is in jail that we may be spared jail. Our problem is merely how to be worthy of so extraordinary a dispensation. It should be elementary for any Christian that he cannot be worthy of that dispensation unless he is himself prepared to go to jail in order that yet others may be spared.

So it goes, as Kurt Vonnegut, in another connection, might have said.

Dorothy Day has been known to despair of our dirty, rotten system. She has been known to simplify the solution for all our afflictions. Pack the jails, she has proclaimed. It is a privilege reserved to those condemned to sanctity to make such statements. For the lot of us the sad fact must be faced that we are not even worthy to pack a jail. We can only each day do what we must do and hope that will somehow slide us by a grace of inadvertence into a worthiness beyond us.

It had become Dan's uncompleted reflection that new forms of community would have to emerge from the contemporary disorder. By that he meant that new forms must be encouraged for all social institutions—for government, for education, for healing, for worship and even, and by no means least, for the family. He had benefited frequently during his underground parabola from close association with families and especially families dominated by that most insurmountable of tyrannies —children. It had been a sobering experience for a priest accustomed to households dominated by God and nuns—in roughly that order. It was his tentative conclusion, I think, that the world could benefit from the experience of the

Church. The exigencies of the times require communities grounded in integers more comprehensive than the single family unit.

During his months of wandering the eastern seaboard, Dan had met often with groups of people concerned to gather. These gatherings had been loosely in the form of what Christians like to call retreats. But the ingathering had been more ambitious than is customary within the caution of Christian tradition. The Body of Christ had been defined so exhaustively as to lack exclusions. Whoever breathed was welcome. No one thought to inquire about individual views of transubstantiation. There were common concerns. There was bread. There was wine. There was even Daniel Berrigan, incidentally a priest. That had seemed sufficient. Had more been provided at the Last Supper? Or less? In a world where men are overwhelmingly reduced to horribly less than sufficient, how could less than sufficient not suffice?

Outreach is a word of late coinage. Dan Berrigan had much hope for the establishments that had erupted of recent years around the enclaves of the military. He delighted in these coffee houses, where misfortunate soldiers might encounter persons who would explore with them the terrible conflicts conscience imposes upon the young. If he were free today to pursue a ministry outside of jail, I have not a doubt that Dan would choose to minister to the victims of the draft. It is those young men whose lives have been placed on the line by old men whose lives have never been on any line. If those of us over thirty have any role left to play, surely it is to erase that line. Let the line be drawn by those who will be asked to die for it. It will then have, I think, an outreach.

Dare we hope in that event there would be *no* line?

One line, however, Daniel Berrigan would draw with all the emphasis at his command. *There must be no violence in the quest for peace.* Dan often spoke of Roger LaPorte, the young man of the Catholic Worker Movement who several years ago set himself afire in front of the United Nations Building and later died after protracted agony. LaPorte's death was a seal for Dan of the senselessness of violence, a sign that violence really is precisely self-defeating. That death could be redemptive only insofar as it served to inform the living of the dignity of nonviolence. The gross violence of the War in Asia renders that war loathsome to a Christian conscience. It must be resisted with a nonviolence every bit as militant as the war itself. The power of death is powerless in the face of the nonviolent intransigence of Christ.

It was Dan's hope that ways could be found to establish communication with the radical left—the Black Panthers, the Weathermen, and others. He admired their intransigence, their courage, their militancy. He did not admire their espousal of violence, neither the overt violence of the Weathermen nor the claim of the Panthers to the right of violence in self-defense. Had he sufficient opportunity, I believe Dan—and Philip— might in time have persuaded the radical left to assume a posture of nonviolence. No greater service could be rendered the radical left and this society at this time than to bring together into one nonviolent community the fractured communities of resistance which make up what small hope remains for the survival of the American experiment. Every bomb exploded by the radical left shatters that hope far more than the murderous rhetoric of the Vice President and more even than the bullets of repression that rhetoric incites.

The movie of *The Train*, meanwhile, overcame incredible obstacles, including obtrusive commercials, and ground its way to a spectacular conclusion. It was succeeded by the news. Daniel and Anthony learned that in Bolivia an American functionary had been abducted and was being held for ransom by a revolutionary group. This led them to speculate what might happen should such tactics be imported to the United States.

They conjured up for their amusement a list of persons who might be abducted. I forget now most of that list but remember having been specially—if perversely—delighted by two nominees: BeBe Rebozo and Billy Graham. Some days later that American hostage was to be barbarously murdered. Kidnap for political ransom entails grave risks of violence that manifestly rules it out as a tactic applicable to a Christian witness against the illegitimacies of the state. For reasons closely allied, Daniel Berrigan had said publicly and privately during his fugitive months that he would never resist or attempt to flee a proximate arrest. Somebody might get hurt or killed.

The morning of Tuesday, August 11 did not dawn. It disclosed instead a roil of clouds and the tempests of a gathering northeast storm. William and Anthony had some breakfast and William repaired to his study to work. Anthony—studyless—bravely attacked a backlog of dirty dishes and watched from the kitchen window the green parrot with the red beak. The winds were strong and ruffled the tropical feathers. The feeder to which the creature clung precariously was anyhow designed for much smaller birds. Green parrot had never seemed more absurd.

So began the incongruities of the day.

Anthony's eyes wandered to a clump of bushes set some distance from the house. There were flashes of orange in the bushes. Scrutiny suggested that the orange was clothing. A man must be in the bushes. Why? Picking berries? There are no berries in those bushes. Watching birds? Odd weather for that. Might it be paranoia on Anthony's part? William Stringfellow would be summoned for an independent observation. There could be no question about it. William also saw a man and the man was orange. Uncle Dan should be roused and invited to comment.

Daniel Berrigan was already roused. He was indeed out by the swimming pool in blue shorts, white shirt and with a towel around his neck. He was in a most particularly exposed position to which he had not before gone. He was looking all about. We hailed him into the house and into the kitchen. He regarded the orange man. An odd color, he said, for an FBI agent to wear on duty. It would be useful to know what the man was doing in the bushes. Why not take the bull by the horns—or the birdwatcher by the binoculars? William would go and ask the man what he was doing in our bushes. It had begun to rain and was shortly to pour. William donned *his* orange (slicker) and sallied forth.

Would it not be possible for Anthony to make Daniel a cup of coffee? Might the coffee be strong? Anthony would try, but his hands had begun to shake. He allowed himself a shot of brandy. Daniel went into the living room and sat on the couch. They did not choose to converse. There was no need to talk. The coffee was not to get made in time. Events were at crescendo.

William Stringfellow approached the orange man. What was he doing in the bushes? He was, he said, birdwatching. In *this* weather? Well, in fact, he was an agent of the FBI. Credentials were ceremoniously displayed. That, said William Stringfellow, may explain why there are now two cars roaring up my driveway. It was agreed that the man in orange and William Stringfellow would walk back to the house. There they could get out of the disintegrating weather. The man in orange was anything but waterproofed.

Daniel and Anthony were also aware of the cars roaring up the driveway. They could also observe other men crawling out from other bushes, some draped in honeysuckle. All the men and the men who exploded out of the cars were dressed casually, as though birdwatching at an island resort. One sported a dampened beret. None was attired for the rain now heavily and gustily engulfing them. The house was surrounded. Anthony allowed himself a second brandy. Daniel still sat upon the couch and said nothing. William and the orange man were now standing among the cars and the birdwatchers outside the front door.

Daniel walked to the door, opened it, and stepped outside. He supposed they wondered who he was. He was Daniel Berrigan. They placed him against the side of one of the cars, handcuffed and frisked him. Then they put him into the car. No weapons were found on Daniel Berrigan. No weapons were drawn by the birdwatchers.

Anthony decided to go outside. Perhaps before they took him away, more suitable clothing might be fetched for Father Berrigan? That, a man with an air of being in charge said, will be allowed. Anthony went to the manger, pausing to explain his mission to its two delicately garbed guardians. He found on top of a pile of bedding a note: CALL JERRY. Dan had apparently spotted birdwatchers before leaving the manger that morning. Or had he left the note there all the time against such an eventuality?

Anthony collected trousers, socks, sneakers, a watch, glasses. That should do it. He started back to the car. A man intercepted him, waving a paper. Anthony should read the paper. He did. It stated his rights. At the bottom was a place for his signature. Did that infer that by signing the paper Anthony would claim those rights? No. Careful reading disclosed that by signing he would waive those rights. The man then read to Anthony the rights he had just read to himself. The man did not read the part about the waiver. Anthony said he did not choose to sign the paper. He told the man his name. He told him where he lived. He admitted he was 42 years old. He gave his weight and his height. He asked the man to look in order to establish the color of his eyes. He said that was all he cared to say. The man was getting wet. It would make sense for him to get out of the rain.

Daniel Berrigan sat in the back seat of the car. Marmaduke

the Christian dog was relieving himself against its left rear tire. A birdwatcher sat next to Dan, handcuffed to him. It seemed apt to Anthony that the birdwatcher should be hand- cuffed to the bird. The clothes and other items were handed in. Daniel looked serene, as though about to set forth on an adventure. The birdwatchers seemed grim, wet, and uncomfort- able. Because of the storm they were shortly to be seasick. Dan was not to be sick only because he had nothing in his stomach to be sick with, not even that strong cup of coffee.

Given the weather, Dan said, perhaps he should have a slicker. William Stringfellow took off his orange slicker and it was handed into the car. Dan became an orange bird. He smiled and said "God Bless."

Omens, as I have said, are idols from which I have yet to sever my belief. It may be that the northeast storm blew him away. I do not know. But we have not seen green parrot from that day to this. Wherever he is we pray someone is keeping an eye on him.

II

THE BERRIGAN WITNESS AS THEOLOGY

JESUS AS A CRIMINAL

Then the whole company of them arose, and
brought him before Pilate. And they began to
accuse him, saying, "We found this man perverting our nation, and forbidding us to give
tribute to Caesar, and saying that he himself is
Christ a king."

LUKE 23.1–2

It is unambiguous in each of the gospel accounts that Jesus
Christ was a criminal.

Of course, it is part of the grandeur of Jesus that many
things may be said of Him. Some of what may be said of Him

Daniel Berrigan continued his ministry at Cornell University while his
Catonsville conviction was being appealed. On October 13, 1969, he presided as liturgist at a service at which William Stringfellow preached this
sermon, having in mind Berrigan's status as a convicted felon.

seems to contradict other things which may be said of Him. That makes it tempting for men to overlook or play down attributes and actions of Jesus which are not congenial to us or convenient for us. Thus, despite what the gospels indicate, it is easy for us to gainsay the criminality of Jesus and to ignore entirely what His status as a criminal may mean for those who profess to affirm and follow Him.

I say that Jesus was, according to the testimonies of the gospels, a criminal: not a mere nonconformist, not just a protester, more than a militant, not only a dissident, not simply a dissenter, but a criminal. More than that, as the Luke passage emphasizes, from the point of view of the State and of the ecclesiastical authorities as well—from the view of the establishment—Jesus was the most dangerous and reprehensible sort of criminal. He was found as one "perverting [the] nation," and "forbidding . . . tribute" to the State. One translation names Jesus a seditionist. In a congressman's jargon, Jesus was a subversive. He was a criminal revolutionary —not one who philosophized about revolution, not a rhetorical revolutionary (such as we hear much nowadays in America), but rather one whose existence threatened the nation in a revolutionary way.

Jesus Christ was, so far as the established authorities and, in the end, so far as the people were concerned, the most loathsome of criminals. And He was so accused, and He was so condemned, and as such He was executed in an aptly ignominious way.

Those Americans who are white, Anglo-Saxon Christians suffer many fantasies about Jesus from the fibs and fairy tales that have been redundantly recited about Him in Sunday schools and from pulpits. Most white churchfolk, for instance, have been brought up to suppose that, in His arrest, trial, and conviction, Jesus was innocent. There is this notion that Jesus was fingered and betrayed by Judas, deserted by His other disciples, and then falsely accused, denied due process of law, and unjustly put to death. Many of us have been taught—wrongly, if the New Testament is credible—to regard Jesus as an ingenuous and hapless victim of a gross miscarriage of justice. But the truth is: He was guilty. Never has a man been apprehended, accused, tried, convicted, sentenced, and executed of whom it may be more certainly avowed: *He was guilty.*

Indeed, as the Luke version attests, far from being a casualty of an abuse of what has come to be called due process of law, there was evidently a serious dispute among the authorities as to where the proper venue lay in the case and as to who had competent jurisdiction over the person of the accused. If anything, it appears that Jesus benefited from more than perfunctory due process. Jesus was in truth treated more conscientiously, as far as due process is concerned—which means, so far as human justice is involved—than, say, Lieutenant Calley or Daniel or Philip Berrigan, a Green Beret or any Black Panther can expect today in America. For Jesus, the justice of both the Roman State and the nation Israel was perfected on the Cross.

Now I mention this—Jesus the guilty criminal, remembering that there are other things to notice about Jesus—in order to make two remarks:

One observation has to do with how it is, in this transaction, that Jesus replaces Barabbas. In the gospels, Barabbas is identified as a convicted murderer and insurrectionist. Barabbas seems to have been some sort of professional revolutionary. Perhaps he was such because of ideological commitment—something like an SDS Weatherman—or perhaps he was a mercenary revolutionary—something like a CIA agent. Or maybe Barabbas was a revolutionary idealist—like Judas, before Judas became disillusioned with Jesus. In any case, Jesus takes the place of Barabbas, the revolutionary, and bears the consequences of Barabbas' revolutionary crimes. This is a remarkable intercession which Jesus thereby enters for all human beings—both the futility and the hope of Barabbas' revolution are exposed and fulfilled in Jesus when He is crucified instead of Barabbas. *All* human revolutions—even those like the Revolution of 1776, which you or I may esteem as glorious—are corruptible in the inception in the vanity by which men suppose they can achieve their own perfection, and yet all human revolutions—including those which threaten a status quo which you or I enjoy—aspire to that very fulfillment of human life in society which Jesus Christ exemplifies.

Jesus was a revolutionary. Barabbas was a revolutionary. But the two are distinguished one from the other. That distinction is illuminated, I think, if we also remember that, while Jesus took the place of Barabbas, Barabbas was released and, in a sense, he replaced Christ. In days alive with ferment called "revolutionary" in this society and elsewhere, the Christian must be alert, and other men must be warned, about the issue of mistaken identity symbolized, in the New Testament, by Barabbas taking the place of Jesus in the world. In the turmoil and excitement of Barabbas' revolution, it is easy to be seduced into supposing that the revolution of Barabbas is actually the revolution of Christ. That temptation is much intensified by the fact that the world can oblige Barabbas' revolution. More concretely, the incumbent political and economic and ideological authorities, in any particular time or place, can accommodate, where they cannot destroy, the factions and ideas that would overthrow them because those revolutionary forces have essentially the same identity and character as do the established powers. That fact does not constitute, in my mind, a persuasive argument against either revolutionary action or revolutionary change; it is just a statement, on one hand, of the most elementary realism about the corruptibility of revolutionary causes and, on the other hand, a theological affirmation about the vitality of death as a moral power in this world affecting all ideologies, all societies, all persons. The Christian must remain aware of how marginal, partial, fragile, transient, and, in the end, literally unrevolutionary the revolutionary cause of Barabbas is. Especially while in the midst of revolution, and even while one risks his reputation or influence or property or life in support of Barabbas' revolution, the Christian must recognize that Barabbas' revolution, as needful as it may be, is not identical with Christ's revolution and is not to be mistaken for Christ's revolution.

The revolution of Christ, as we behold in the exchange of places between Christ and Barabbas, is not a revolution which the world can abide. There is, in other words, an immense, radical, and generic difference between the Christian as revolutionary and any other revolutionaries. Revolution manifest in Jesus Christ does not have an idealistic or ideological or, least of all, a mercenary character. It has, rather, an empirical character: the Christians (not mere churchgoers, but the *Christians*) have had some experience of suffering death in this world—the death which is a moral power; the death which is at work within a man, between a man and himself, among men, between and among men and institutions; the death which is the idol of nations—and the Christians have known the transcendence of death's assaults, politically as much as personally, so that they live unintimidated by the continuing, ingenious, and versatile aggressions of death. The mark that distinguishes a Christian (which, by the way, has nothing to do with either religion or rectitude) is that he has endured, already, a reconciliation of his own life with the world, so that conflict, injustice, alienation, brutality, moral confusion, or any other portents of death are no longer an intimidation, enticement, enslavement, a threat or defeat for him. The mark of the Christian is, simply, that he is a matured and freed human being. The direct political implication of this risen character of the Christian is that, as contrasted with other revolutionaries, of which Barabbas is the example and symbol, the Christian is an incessant revolutionary. He is always, everywhere, in revolt—not for himself but for humanity. There is something inherently, invariably, persistently, perpetually, inexhaustibly, inevitably revolutionary in the suffering of reconciliation—in the experience of one's own personhood as humanity in society—which constitutes the Christian life in this world. The Christian as revolutionary is constantly welcoming the gift of human life, for himself and for all men, by exposing, opposing, and overturning all that betrays, entraps, or attempts to kill human life. The difference between Christ and Barabbas as revolutionaries is the difference between life and death as both the imminent reality and the ultimate value of revolution.

This issue is dramatized, for us Americans today, poignantly in the American Revolution which, from the New Testament perspective, was a revolution of Barabbas and not a revolution of Christ, despite what either Pilgrims or politicians have said. We who are Americans witness in this hour the exhaustion of the American revolutionary ethic. Wherever we turn, that is what is to be seen: in the ironic public policy of internal colonialism symbolized by the victimization of the welfare population, in the usurpation of the federal budget—and, thus, the sacrifice of the nation's material and moral necessities—by an autonomous military-scientific-intelligence principality, by the police aggressions against black citizens, by political prosecutions of dissenters, by official schemes to intimidate the media and vitiate the First Amendment, by cynical designs to demean and neutralize the courts. Yet the corruption of the American revolutionary ethic is not a recent or sudden problem. It has been inherent and was, in truth, portended in the very circumstances in which the Declaration of Independence was executed. To symbolize that, white men who subscribed to that cause at the same time countenanced the institutionalization in the new nation of chattel slavery and many were themselves owners of slaves. That incomprehensible hypocrisy in America's revolutionary origins foretells the contemporary decadence of the revolutionary tradition in the U.S.A.

The second matter I wish to mention, apart from the contrast between the work of death in revolutions like that of Barabbas and the perpetual revolutionary action of the Christian, is the relation of the State, and of established society, to Jesus Christ.

It is instructive, as to the disposition of the conventional churches in this country now, to note that, according to the biblical accounts, the ecclesiastical authorities, for all practical purposes, acted as servants of the State in the confrontation with Jesus. In one version, the chief priests protest: "Caesar is our king, we have no other king but Caesar." In the dispute over jurisdiction between Pilate and Herod, they warn: "If you release Him you will not be Caesar's friend." The ecclesiastics were, practically speaking, surrogates of the State. That is an all-too-familiar situation for chief priests to be found in. That was also the situation in Nazi Germany. It was similar, Kierkegaard says, in Scandinavia about a century ago. It is that way, notoriously, with the Dutch Reformed Church in the Union of South Africa. It has been the role of white Anglo-Saxon denominations in most jurisdictions in this land, both before and since the Civil War. On the issues of race and war —which is to say, on virtually all issues—the white churches and sects can be fairly viewed as the religious arm of the political establishment at the present time, or, the same can be viewed the other way around—the incumbent national administration represents a kind of corny fulfillment of the profoundly secular character of white Protestant denominationalism in America.

When I now speak of the State, therefore, the reference includes the inherited ecclesiastical authorities and institutions, just as much as one notices the guilty association of the chief priests and Caesar's interest in the trial of Jesus.

Why is there this terrible hostility between the State and Christ? Why is Jesus so threatening to the nation? Why is He found to be criminal?

The answer to such questions is in the indictment: He says that "He himself is Christ a king."

The kingship of Jesus Christ possesses extraordinary connotations. On the cross, remember, the charge affixed over His head read: "King of the Jews." By the virtue of Israel's election and vocation as the people of God, as the holy nation, as the pioneer of mankind in reconciliation—a calling which is not revoked despite any apostasy of Israel—the King of the Jews is the King of humanity. The kingship of Christ not only exceeds the authority of Caesar but it surpasses all aspirations for new or wiser or better kings of Barabbas' revolution. The kingship of Christ means Christ as Man—mature Man, fulfilled Man, whole Man, true Man—ruling the whole of time and creation. The kingship of Christ means, as Paul saw it, Christ as Second Adam—as Man (again, as it were) exercising dominion in history over all creatures (including all principalities and powers, institutions and ideologies, corporations and nations), over the whole of nature, over all things whatsoever. Christ as king means Man no more enslaved to institutions, no longer a pawn of technologies, no mere servant of the State or of any other authority, no incapacitated victim of a damaged environment. Christ as King means Man free from bondage to ideologies and institutions, free from revolutionary causes as well, free from idolatry of Caesar, and, not the least of it free from religion which tries to disguise such slaveries as virtuous, free from all these and all similar claims which really only conceal death—only the dehumanization of life—for men.

The authorities of Rome and of an apostate Israel perceived quite accurately that Christ as king threatened them poignantly and urgently. Christ as king embodies an unrelenting revolutionary threat to each and every nation and, paradoxically, to all revolutions within any nation as they become incarnations of the power of death feigning to be the definitive moral power in history.

According to the biblical witness, death is not the decisive moral power in history, but it is the *only* moral power the State (or any other principalities) can invoke as a sanction against human beings and against human life as such. That is, also, plainly to be seen now in this nation: death is the moral power upon which the State relies when it removes citizens from society for preventive detention or other political imprisonment, or when it estops free speech, or when it militarizes the police, or when it drives youth into exile, or when it confines millions in black ghettos and consigns millions more to malnutrition and illiteracy, or when it manipulates inflation and credit to preoccupy, demoralize, and thereby conform the middle classes, or when it purchases grapes or lettuce to covertly break a strike, or when it collusively abets a governor's defiance of the courts, or when it hunts priests as fugitives.

No wonder, in the earlier circumstances, when the State confronted Christ the king—Christ the free human being—that it should find Him a criminal and send Him to the cross.

And no wonder, at this moment, in this country, where the power of death is so militant in the universities, in the corporate structures, in the churches, in the labor movement, in the political institutions, in the Pentagon, in the business of science, in the technological order, in the environment itself, in the realms of ideology, in the State, that, as with Jesus, the Christian, living as a free man, living in transcendence of death's power, living, thus, as an implacable, insatiable, unappeasable, tireless, and resilient revolutionary, should be regarded by all authorities as a criminal.

As in the time of the trial of Jesus Christ, so in this day and place, to truly be a free man is to be a criminal.

AN AUTHORITY OVER DEATH

As I regard myself, I have never been especially religious, and, having been reared as an Episcopalian, the pietism of which I may be guilty has been ambiguous—a casual matter and an inconvenience more than a matter of consistency or fixed conviction. Still, as a younger person, particularly while an undergraduate, I had been precocious theologically, and instead of being attentive to whatever it was that students, in those days, may have been interested in, I concentrated much, in the privacy of my mind, on theology and upon what might be called theologizing.

I do not mean that I often studied or even read the works

St. John's Episcopal Church in Northampton, Massachusetts, is the congregation in which William Stringfellow was reared. The Berrigan capture on Block Island caused much concern in that parish, and on October 20, 1970, Stringfellow delivered the sermon which follows to the congregation in Northampton.

of theologians, because I did not do that, but I did begin then to read the Bible, in an unordered and spontaneous way, and I did begin, thus, to be caught up in a dialectic between an experience with the biblical witness and my everyday existence as a human being. I recall, in this, that there seemed to me to be a strong opposition between both the biblical story and my own life, on one side, and religion and religious moralism, on the other. After a while that opposition took on greater clarity, and I could discern that the former has to do with living humanly, while the latter has to do with dying in a moral sense and, indeed, with dying in *every* sense.

To anyone who knows this about me, it will come as no surprise to learn that in the immediate aftermath of the seizure by the federal authorities of Daniel Berrigan, at Eschaton, the home that Anthony Towne and I share on Block Island, I spent what time our suddenly hectic circumstances would afford with the New Testament. This was no exercise in solace; neither Anthony nor I had any regret or grief to be consoled, and we had each beheld the serenity of Dan as he was taken into the anxious custody of the FBI. The coolness of Berrigan had been a startling contrast to the evident shame and agitation of the agents, and we both understood that, whatever Dan was suffering in his transition from fugitive to captive, he had no need for pity or remorse, least of all from us.

To open, then, the Bible was an obvious, straightforward, natural thing to do. Berrigan had done something similar, publicly, when he preached to the Germantown congregation, relying upon texts from the Letter to the Hebrews. It is a wholly characteristic recourse for Christians, since, in the Bible, they find a holy history which is human history transfigured and since, in turn, they realize that human history is holy history and since, thus, they dwell in the continuity of the biblical word and the present moment.

Through the late spring and the summer, I had been engaged with the Babylon passages in the Book of Revelation, and that effort had influenced my participation in the conversations which were taking place with Daniel and Anthony. With the abrupt interruption of our talk on August 11th, I put aside—though not out of ready reach—the Babylon texts to return to the Acts of the Apostles and to some of the Letters that are thought to be chronologically proximate to Acts, specifically James and First Peter.

These testimonies, of course, deal with the issues of the Apostolic Church struggling to distinguish itself from the sects of Judaism, while at the same time confronting the political claims and challenges of the zealots, on one hand, and the manifest blasphemy and idolatry of the civic religion of Rome, on the other. All these subjects are so familiar in contemporary American reference that it is a temptation to treat them fatalistically (pursuing trite queries, such as, *Is Nixon our Nero?*).

The immediate trauma of the aggression against our household, in which Dan had been taken, spared me from speculations of that sort, however, and I realized while reading Acts that more rudimentary and more fundamental problems had to be faced. I remembered vividly, moreover, how the same matters had plagued and confounded me, years earlier, for all my precocity, and how, in a sense, the situation of August 11th, 1970, had been long since foreshadowed. The episode of the arrest of Peter and John, as told in Acts, following upon the healing of the lame beggar at the temple gate, sums up the issues:

> *And as they were speaking to the people, the priests and the captain of the temple and the Sadducees came upon them, annoyed because they were teaching the people and proclaiming in Jesus the resurrection from the dead. And they arrested them and put them in custody . . .*
>
> Acts 4.1–3a

I read this and read it and read it; the most difficult questions of my initiation in Bible study returned: *What does "the resurrection from the dead" mean if proclaiming it is cause for arrest? Why is healing a cripple so threatening and provocative to the public authorities? Why should this apparent good work count as a crime?*

This arrest of Peter and John, associated publicly with the healing of the lame man and the open preaching of the resurrection, portended a wider persecution of Christians and an official repression of the Gospel, but it also relates back to the reasons for the condemnation and execution of Jesus, in which, it must not be overlooked, Jesus' own ministry of healing was interpreted by the incumbent authorities as if it were political agitation and was deemed by them to be a threat to their political authority. Where healing or, more broadly, where the witness to the resurrection is involved, the comprehension and response of Caesar and his surrogates to Christ as well as to the Apostles is, significantly, consistent. Such a witness is judged as a crime against the State.

There is a sentimentalistic (and unbiblical) tradition of "bible stories" in American Christendom which, when coupled with the thriving naïveté of Americans toward their own nation, renders it difficult for many citizens, particularly churchfolk, to assimilate the fact that the Christian witness is treated as a criminal offense, even though this is so bluntly and repeatedly reported in New Testament texts. Within the American churchly ethos, biblical references to healing, however they may be interpreted medically, as metaphors or magic or miracles, are generally supposed to be highly private, individual, and personal happenings, having nothing categorically to do with politics. Meanwhile, when it comes to the resurrection as an event and the meaning of the resurrection as the gist of the Gospel, the sentimentalization of Scripture has reached a quintessence of distortion, so that to regard the resurrection in a political context, as the New Testament does, seems a most radical incongruity: an unthinkable thought.

At the same time, the simplistic Constantinianism which informs American attitudes toward Christianity and the nation allows Americans to view Rome and the ancillary ecclesiastical-political establishment allowed in the Empire at the time of the Crucifixion and during the Apostolic era as an aberrant version of the State rather than as an archtypical symbol of all political institutions and authorities in any time or place. There are no doubt some serious distinctions to be kept between Rome and America or between the Nazi State and the United States or between Sweden and the U.S.A. or, for that matter, between Revolutionary America and contemporary America, but such issues must not obscure the truth that every nation, every political regime, every civil power shares a singular characteristic which outweighs whatever may be said to distinguish one from another. And it is *that* common attribute of the State as such to which the New Testament points where the texts deal with the witness in Christ being condemned as criminal.

The sanction—though it takes different forms, it is, in principle, the *only* sanction—upon which the State relies is death. In the healing episodes, as in other works within the ministry in Christ, as in the proclamation of the resurrection from the dead, the authority of Christ over the moral power of death is verified as well as asserted. It is this claim of the Gospel which the State beholds as threatening; it is the audacity to verify this claim in living—in thought and word and action— that the State condemns as crime. The preaching of the resurrection, far from being politically innocuous, and the healing incidents, instead of being merely private, are profound, even cosmic, political acts.

This is how, on August 11th, in the hours soon after Father Berrigan's capture and incarceration, I thought of Dan's min-

istry and the various ways in which he has exercised his vocation through the years that Anthony and I have known him:
as prisoner, as guest, as fugitive, as convicted felon, as Catonsville defendant, as exile, as citizen in protest, as poet, as priest
—as a man. Confronted with what I was reading in Acts, I
marveled at the patience of Berrigan's witness; I sensed the
humor of what he has said and done being construed, especially in the churches, as so radical. It seemed utterly obvious
that Berrigan had taken his stand in the mainstream of the
Apostolic tradition and that his course had been not at all
unusual but simply normative.

I do not imply that Berrigan is engaged in some self-con-
scious imitation of Peter or John or any other of the earlier
Christians; I simply mean that to proclaim the resurrection in
word and act is an affront which the State cannot tolerate
because the resurrection exposes the subservience of the State
to death as the moral purpose of the society which the State
purports to rule. As has been intimated, the clarity or literal-
ness with which the moral dependence upon death of the
State can be discerned may vary much, from time to time and
from place to place, but, nonetheless, the American circumstances today represent an instance in which death is pervasive,
aggressive, and undisguised in its moral domination of the
nation's existence. Theologically speaking, the war in Vietnam
is not just an improvident, wicked, or stupid venture, but it
epitomizes the militancy and insatiability of death as a moral
power reigning in the nation—as that morality in relation
to which everything and everyone is supposedly judged and
justified. Thus to oppose the war becomes much more than a
difference over policy. From the viewpoint of the State, protest against the war undermines the *only* moral purpose which
the State has—the work of death—and risks the only punishment of which the State is capable: consignment to death or to
some status which embodies the same meaning as death—

though it be short of execution—like imprisonment, prosecution, persecution, loss of reputation or property or employment, intimidation to beget silence and conformity.

To those who may think this a grotesque doctrine of the State in America in the present day, I cite, amidst a growing accumulation of other evidence, what happened in the case of the Catonsville Nine to the Berrigan brothers and their fellow defendants. Verbal protests against the war, and all it symbolizes, had been of little or no avail, and these citizens had dramatized the issue by destroying draft records with napalm, taking effective precautions against their action causing violence or any harm to human beings, since that would vitiate their witness against the violence of the State. Let it be conceded that the State could not overlook the incident (although, in fact, the State frequently does exactly that in circumstances where its dignity is as much embarrassed). One option for the State would have been to prosecute the defendants on nominal or minimal charges. There exists ample precedent for that and, if that had been done, the authority of the State would have been asserted in a way which recognized the political and, indeed, theatrical, character of the action—as distinguished from one implementing criminal intent—and, it can be argued, the State might then have succeeded in stopping similar protests by minimizing their notoriety. Instead, the State reacted to what the Catonsville Nine had done as if it were a crime of magnitude. Precedent was put aside, along with common sense, and legal process was usurped for a political objective, namely, the quashing of dissent. The manner in which the State undertook the prosecution of the Catonsville Nine betrays a purpose not only to punish the defendants harshly but also to admonish all citizens, emphatically, to be quiet, to behave, to acquiesce, for fear that otherwise they risk a similar retribution.

The intimidating message of the Catonsville prosecution,

furthermore, does not stand out alone but is just one of very many other recent pathetic aggressions of the State against citizens, the most urgent of which the Black Panthers have suffered.

In the days that followed upon Dan's capture, many Block Island neighbors, many other friends, and many strangers have told Anthony and myself of their outrage and their apprehension—whatever they might think of what the Catonsville Nine did or of Father Berrigan's fugitive interlude—that the State seemed so anxious and overreactive and was in such hot pursuit of, as one person put it, "a harmless man." In this tentative, uneasy perception, I believe, a host of citizens, otherwise passive, grasp the desperate issue in what is taking place in America now: the power of death incarnate in the State violating, enslaving, perverting, imprisoning, destroying human life in society. To fail or refuse to act against this amounts to an abdication of one's humanness, a renunciation of the gift of one's own life, as well as a rejection of the lives of other human beings, a very ignominious idolatry of death. In the face of that the only way no matter how the State judges or what the State does—is to live in the authority over death which the resurrection is. A person cannot be human and be silent about that, as *Acts* attests:

> So they called them and charged them not to speak or teach at all in the name of Jesus. But Peter and John answered them, "Whether it is right in the sight of God to listen to you rather than to God, you must judge; for we cannot but speak of what we have seen and heard."
>
> Acts 4.18–20

WHO ARE THE PRISONERS?

During his most recent visit to Block Island, Daniel Berrigan asked to hear the tape made at St. Clement's Church exactly a year ago today, of the requiem for James A. Pike.

We listened to the recording—Dan and Anthony Towne and myself. It has since been a small comfort to me, as perhaps it will also be to this congregation, to realize that in this way the federal authorities may inadvertently have been afforded opportunity to overhear the mass and music and homily given here for Bishop Pike a few days after he had been found dead in the Judean desert.

The first public remarks about Dan Berrigan's apprehension on Block Island by William Stringfellow were at a mass for prisoners of conscience celebrated at St. Clement's Church in New York City on September 20, 1970. Exactly a year earlier, Stringfellow had preached in the same congregation at a requiem mass for the late Bishop James A. Pike.

(The original tape of that service, I regret, is of low technical quality, and, in the circumstances, it has occurred to me that the FBI—which has its only undisputed competence in electronic surveillance—may have obtained an improved recording, the public release of which might be had if an appropriate court order were sought.)

Hearing the Pike requiem—however it may have affected prospective intruders—moved Berrigan and Towne and myself to remembrances of Jim and, in contrast to those reminiscences, into conversation about the great silent majority of the ecclesiastical hierarchy in the churches of this land, about the character of the incumbent public authorities and of the State as such in America, and about the tactics of witness for Christians and for other serious human beings in days such as these.

I purpose this morning, in this mass celebrated for prisoners of conscience, to recount some of what was affirmed amongst the three of us in that conversation in order to make emphatic why the capture of Daniel Berrigan, while a misfortune, is not demoralizing either for him and other similar prisoners, or for any of the rest of us who care for human life in society. A year ago, in this place, there was a reason for a requiem. There is no reason for a requiem this morning; in truth it behooves an anniversary of a requiem for Bishop Pike to carry on the celebration of life.

Dan Berrigan's own most recent recollection of Jim Pike, as he mentioned after hearing the tape, concerned Pike's exuberant presence at the trial of the Catonsville Nine in Baltimore. As special counsel, Pike had been in court with the other lawyers and he had brainstormed with them and with the defendants about the strategy of the case. As a bishop, he had addressed the throng of supporters of the Nine who, during the course of the proceedings gathered nightly, as if they were a congregation, in a nearby church. Pike's sense of episcopal vocation, as well as his commitment as a lawyer, which authorized his public identification with the accused, stood out in poignant contrast to the quietism which generally prevailed among other bishops and archbishops at the time, save for one Roman prelate who, on the eve of the trial, had declared publicly that he "washed his hands" of the accused, a remark which caused Pike to speculate with Dan about whether the archbishop in question could have been prompted by reading the New Testament.

This disassociation of an archbishop from the defendants, all of whom are Christians and all of whom had avowed their action as an intentioned witness, and the generally prevalent silence of the hierarchy, whether occasioned by indifference, hostility, or default, came as no surprise to anybody. We have become accustomed in America to expect little more than a platitudinous social witness from bishops, save where some vested interest of the churchly institutions is at stake. Surprise, rather, attaches to a bishop such as James A. Pike had been, one whose social conscience was not suspended by elevation to the episcopacy and whose public voice was not inhibited but increased in Apostolic office.

"Why are there no bishops in jail?" Berrigan had asked, in the conversation that followed upon our listening to the tape of the Pike requiem at St. Clement's. It was no rhetorical question. Dan was not complaining that pharisees so far outnumber prophets in the ranks of contemporary prelates; he had been instead, talking about the extremely dehumanizing changes being wrought in America today, which the war and white supremacy and the militarization of the police and the politicizing of legal process respectively and jointly epitomize, and he was lamenting the pastoral failure of bishops, in all the churches, to squarely confront such realities.

The precedents for imprisoned bishops are venerable. In the emerging church of First Century Christianity it was the pastoral vigilance—not the prophetic vision—of the Apostles and their earliest successors that provoked very many arrests and imprisonments and not a few executions. The peace symbol which is worn today derives from the upside-down cross upon which some were crucified. Peter and John, Paul and Barnabas, James, the brother of Jesus—their roster is illustrious and long and includes, it must be mentioned on these premises, toward the end of the first century, during the second official persecution of the Christians, St. Clement. Of course, we have regarded their actions, which placed them in trouble with the political authorities, with condescension, and we have romanticized their sufferings as prisoners of conscience and as victims of the State so that we could dismiss their examples as irrelevant to us in this nation at this time.

I heard another Jesuit recently boast of a similar evasion of the issues raised by Father Berrigan's conduct. "Dan is a poet," he said, accusingly, not only as if nonpoets are categorically excused from humanity but also as if that fact about Dan somehow neutralized the brutalization of life or justified overlooking the totalitarianization of society against which Berrigan acted. The State, meanwhile, engages in an equivalent deception: by rendering those citizens who protest anonymous and voiceless as prisoners, it seeks to suppress the truth which the protests expose. That Berrigan, on behalf of himself, but as much on behalf of his brother, held hostage so long in the Lewisburg dungeons, and on behalf of all prisoners of conscience, refused to be taken in by grandiloquent sophistry of the authorities by remaining so notoriously at large no doubt explains the overkill by which the State hunted him.

Berrigan has acted, we have reason to be grateful, in a way which does not allow to any but the morally insane the indulgence of ignoring the issues. And, for that matter, the realities for the First Century Christians—when so many bishops were jailed and killed, and, then, when common be-

lievers were driven underground, and, later, when the persecu-
tions became public spectacles, diverting the people from the
State's usurpation of their humanity—do not furnish the convenience of being different from our situation in the Twentieth
Century. In the earlier era there was widespread and accelerat-
ing social agitation which erupted in certain provinces as
episodic anarchy and which eventually radicalized as open
revolution. The causes of discontent were various and complicated, aggravated by that neglect which is a sort of vanity
to which incumbent leaders are peculiarly vulnerable, and
multiplied by each attempt to repress dissidence. A focus
for these troubles was the accommodation instituted between
Rome and Israel by which the religion of the Jews was accorded official recognition and allowed to coexist alongside
the civic religion of the Empire so long as it remained politically innocuous, save in a negative sense, in which the practice
of religion consumed the time and energies of people sufficiently to make them complacent or apathetic about politics.
The seal and sanction of this guilty bargain between the
ruling authorities and the ecclesiastical establishment was
an infamous tax which the dutiful religious were required to
pay—the same tax, by the way, which occasioned the journey
of Joseph and the pregnant Mary to Bethlehem to be enrolled.

The tax became a symbol of oppression, of the perversion of
the biblical faith, of an unwarranted control of life by the
State, of power abused so consistently as to be illegitimatized,
of death as social purpose. A zealotic party arose from Judaism
to oppose and protest and, in the end, to seek to overthrow
by violence this regime and to depose those who collaborated
with it. The ministry of Jesus and, then, after Pentecost, the
witness of the Apostolic Church and that of the early post-
Apostolic congregations took place in the midst of this
gathering turbulence. For the church a dilemma was posed
between being stifled as a sect of Judaism under the pro-

tective custody of the Roman State or becoming accessories to the zealots. To do the first was bound to provoke the wrath of the zealots; to do the second risked official persecution. But to do either betrayed the Gospel of Jesus Christ. Despite periods of vacillation, attempts at appeasement, and much temporizing, before the century ended the Christians had so significantly distinguished themselves from both the religious establishment and the professional revolutionaries that they suffered the aggressions of both.

This had, of course, been foreshadowed in Jesus' ministry and was implicit in the confrontation between Jesus and the chief priests when they questioned Him about giving "tribute to Caesar." The accounts in the New Testament all refer to this interrogation as a trick or hypocrisy or a test to which the ecclesiastics sought to impose on Jesus. Indeed it was. Whether to pay taxes to Caesar concealed the fundamental political issue of the day: acquiescence and subservience, or resistance and revolution. In the face of this kind of challenge, the response of Jesus is to raise an even more rudimentary problem to the identity and character of Caesar in relation to the sovereignty of God: "Then render to Caesar the things that are Casear's, and to God the things that are God's." Bluntly, Jesus puts the issue of the legitimacy of the State, not merely constitutionally but vocationally. Is the State stupidly and blindly, in humiliation of their humanity, an idol which men serve or a servant of men for the enhancement of human life in society? The answer to that, with respect to the State, in a specific time and place, determines whether *anything* belongs to Caesar.

Jesus left his inquisitors "marveling at his answer," and it was only as they readied the Crucifixion for Him that they fathomed that the tribute which Caesar then required was idolatry, and that Jesus had forbidden that. And later on, with brave anguish, the First Century Christians were enabled to be faithful to Jesus when they were threatened in similar ways.

In America today these issues claim every one of us, and they are attended still with deception and confusion. Part of that is the notion that conformity to the views of our so-called leaders, and automatic submission to the demands of officers and operatives of the State, despite any coincident abuse of power or denial of due process, is somehow transposed into a test of loyalty to the nation. Exactly the opposite is the case: a loyal esteem for the nation requires resistance to the illegitimacies of Presidents, as well as policemen. Anthony and I were dismayed to learn, in the aftermath of the Berrigan capture, that the FBI had, among other measures, taken up a watch of our household from some property adjacent to, though some distance from, Eschaton, because the owner supposed that "the FBI can go anywhere it wants to." It is, I believe, such apprehensiveness toward the State and toward the attaches of the State that chiefly undermines the rule of law in this land and displaces it with a rule of violence and intimidation so drastically consummated in the war and in official aggressions against those who protest the war.

Meanwhile, there is the problem symbolized in the First Century by the zealots. The relationship between the Christians and the zealots is poignant because the Christians, faced with the reality of a decadent and repressive State, discern, as lucidly as the zealots, the pathetic need for change of revolutionary magnitude and scope. Yet the Christian pauses over the tactics of the zealots. Revolutionary violence which overthrows the violence of the State can itself only become a regime of violence. Tactics cannot be severed from ethics, and imitation of the enemy is the most common way in which ideology has been confounded, idealism corrupted, and revolutions rendered futile. The Christian perseveres in nonviolent actions of protest and resistance—shunning whatever increases the work of death—in the hope of thereby calling into being new forms of life in society. And if, sometimes, as in the First Century, that means the Christian becomes as much a victim of the hostility and assault of the zealots as of the State, then so be it.

"Why are there no bishops in jail?"

A way to answer that is: Bishop Pike is dead.

Anyway, the Berrigans, at last, are both in prison. Beside them are many, many more who have been jailed, who live now in jeopardy of political prosecution, who have been driven into exile, who are numbered as deserters, who risk courts-martial, or who are locked in ghettos or consigned to a nomad existence.

These are all prisoners—all political prisoners—in America, it seems. Yet if death holds no fear for them, then neither does any imprisonment, and though they look like prisoners, they remain free men.

There are other prisoners in this land, though on first appearances they do not look like prisoners. They are the ones who are so afraid of death—so apprehensive for their own survival—that they do not know how to live as human beings. They are imprisoned by the fear of jail or of disgrace or loss of "security." They forfeit their minds to official lies; they vacate their consciences; they surrender to intimidation. They are the real prisoners in this country—they and those who call themselves our leaders and who exercise the State's authority with such guile and savagery that their own humanity is devoured.

This is a mass for prisoners. It is, like any mass, a celebration of the gift of life. I invite you, as you participate in this celebration, to behold how the nominal prisoners—the ones in jail—intercede for the humanity of those who have put them in jail who are more certainly prisoners in our midst.

THE STATE, THE CHURCH, AND THE REALITY OF CONSCIENCE

In the arena in which theology, ethics, and law confront one another—which designates, of course, the realm of God's judgment of men and nations and is, thus, appropriately mysterious—no question is more venerable or recurrent or ambiguous than that of the vocation of the Church of Christ in relation to the law and to society. It is not an issue about which there has been either much coherence or much consistency. That is evident now on the American scene, where we have beheld the State—without benefit of due process—holding a priest—Philip Berrigan—hostage in solitary confinement in order to force the surrender of his brother—Daniel Berrigan —also a priest, who styled himself an "outlaw for peace" and a "fugitive from injustice," while, simultaneously, we

At the 1970 national convention of the Canon Law Society of America, held in New Orleans, William Stringfellow gave this paper.

have heard the president of the American Bar Association mount a Baptist pulpit to berate the churches for abetting lawlessness.

This matter seems always to have been attended by controversy and contradiction. The contemporary realities of church-state relations in Brazil, in China, in South Africa, in Greece dramatize that. The sadducean contrivance to morally rationalize the Nazi regime—an effort that lasted until the Second World War was certain—and the poignant refutation of that in actions of Bonhoeffer and the confessing movement stand as a classic instance in point in this century, so far. In earlier times, the intricacy of the issue of church, law, and society was primary in the Reformation—especially in its Geneva version. Need one, in these presents, cite the Inquisition? Or recall one principal source of the ambiguity—in the Constantinian Arrangement? Though we sometimes like to romanticize the Apostolic Church and to regard it as a lucid, if neglected, precedent, the truth is that the Apostles and their initial successors in the First Century Church were apprehensive, equivocal, inconsistent, and confused about what constituted fidelity to the Gospel in the practical relationships of the Church to the law and to the needs of society.

As both a practicing Christian and a practicing lawyer, I have tended to see and deal with the question in terms of specific cases, especially those in my Harlem work and in others involving dissenters or similar outcasts. Lately, since the capture of Father Daniel Berrigan on Block Island, this tendency has become even more pronounced. As a precaution against overpersonalization of the issue, there are reflections upon the relevance of the First Epistle of Peter, mindful of the consternation which afflicted the early Christians, at the time this Letter was composed, about church, law, and society, but believing that we can be edified despite that circumstance, and, indeed, *because* of it.

Be subject for the Lord's sake to every human institution, whether it be to the emperor as supreme, or to governors as sent by him to punish those who do wrong and to praise those who do right. For it is God's will that by doing right you should put to silence the ignorance of foolish men. Live as free men, yet without using your freedom as a pretext for evil; but live as servants of God. Honor all men. Love the brotherhood. Fear God. Honor the emperor.

1 Peter 2.13–17

Honor the emperor—that seems a straightforward instruction uncomplicated by entendre and sufficiently emphatic. And, just so, it has been often interpreted—particularly by emperors and their military, political, commercial, and ecclesiastical attachés at court or in cabinet—as an unconditioned requirement of allegiance and obedience to the *occupant* of office, as distant from the office or institution itself or from the State as such. There are from time to time extraordinary reigns, like Nero's (during which the Apostle whose name this letter bears was executed) or, later, Domitian's rule (when the official persecution of Christians reached the proportions of massacre), or, in modern times, Franco's regime or, one supposes, Mao's China—in which incumbent and office are merged. In such circumstances, the superficial version of this text—*honor the emperor*—has yielded astounding consequences, such as the pretext for the acquiescence of Hitler's bishops and clergy to the incineration of eight million Jews.

The biblical context does not support a simplistic transliteration of *honor the emperor* as automatic obeisance either to the emperor or to acts of policies carried out in the name of Caesar. Indeed, any view such as that must be deemed an abuse of the biblical statement if notice is taken that the phrase *honor the emperor* is modified by the sentence *Be subject for the Lord's sake to every human institution.* That to which honor is due is the office, not the occupant of the office, with the necessary inference that the incumbent is worthy of honor only insofar as he acts within the discipline of the institution. A Christian, following the counsel of First Peter, might well be found opposing the emperor and exposing the illegitimacy of the actions and policies of the emperor in order to *honor the emperor,* in order, in other words, to elucidate and uphold the vocation of the emperor. I remind you that we know of a grave instance of such an audacious and ironic witness in Dietrich Bonhoeffer.

More than that, in the situation prevailing when this letter of Peter was composed, in Rome, there were Christians in the congregation there—specifically, some who in their secular status were slaves or otherwise dispossessed—who were implicated deeply in challenging the legitimacy of the emperor's rule. Their radical social concern seems, significantly, to have been as much responsive to the agitation of the zealotic faction of Judaism—which was motivated by revolutionary idealism but advocated violent rebellion and practiced terrorism—as to the abuses and outrages of the emperor and his administration. Officially, the Church at this time, toward the end of the Apostolic era, was deemed by the political authorities to be one of the Jewish sects entitled to legal recognition or, as some might think of it, restricted in protective custody. It was a dubious status (affecting such substantive matters for the Gospel as the missionary outreach to the Gentiles), a kind of comity by which the State allowed a practice of religion so long as it remained political, innocuous and did not disturb the pagan idolatries. By the time this letter was written, this entente between Rome and the Jewish sects was breaking up, in part because of the boldness of the zealots, partly because the civic religion had come to be construed as worship of the emperor, also because the ecumenical—and, thus, political—character of the Christian faith was becoming more prominent and because the eschatological hope was beginning to be comprehended by Christians not as some nebulous promise to be passively awaited but as a lively hope (to use Peter's phrase) to be embodied and verified in the transfiguration of the common life of human beings in society here and now.

This tumult in Rome foreshadowed the turmoil that before the end of the First Century was to engulf the whole Empire. Still, when this letter was written, the Christians in the provinces of Asia Minor, to whom it was addressed, had not yet suffered persecution, although they did endure slanderous accusations, constant surveillance, and intermittent police harassment. The letter, intended to be read in the celebration of the sacrament of baptism, expounds the new citizenship in Christ, in contrast to the old citizenship under Caesar. One speculates whether Peter was trying to warn the Christians in the hinterlands of what was portended for them in the aggressions against human beings which were taking place in Rome. Perhaps he sought some kind of accommodation with authority exercised illegitmately to secure safety for the provincial Christians, though that, I suggest, is unlikely just because of the letter's context in baptism. Whatever the case, any conceivable motive of Peter to compromise on the issue of the legitimacy of the emperor or the office or the acts and policies carrying the emperor's name and authority in order to obviate the prospective persecution was futile, as Peter's own execution—in a manner customarily reserved for terrorists —shows.

Should this all sound familiar?

I think it should.

It does seem familiar if one has been attentive to the cases of the Berrigan brothers—not to mention any others, despite the fact that prisons in this country hold many others of whom, though they be less conspicuous than the Berrigans, one could speak as urgently.

The public action of the Berrigans starts out as a protracted patient, peaceful, reasoned, conscientious, verbal protest against illegitimate policies of successive presidential administrations that have entrapped the nation in the most vainglorious war of all: depleting its youth, subverting its conscience, destroying its community, squandering its wealth, manipulating its majority classes, usurping the Constitution, despoiling the earth in Southeast Asia, mutilating the children there, corrupting other nations as mercenaries, both at home and abroad flaunting contempt for human life, everywhere profiting only death.

The complaint goes unheeded. Again and again the war escalates. The credibility of government is solemnly impaired.

The dissent finds theatrical expression. Pieces of official paper are destroyed with napalm to dramatize the moral insanity of burning people with napalm.

Now the witness is noticed by political authority turned apprehensive and vindictive by the very abuse of the power of the State which is the proximate cause of the war and the multifarious consequences of the war. All citizens—everyone—must be shown by the way these priests are prosecuted and punished that the only allowable responses to illegitimate authority are acquiescence or silence or conformity or obeisance. So the Berrigans, along with the other defendants, are tried and treated in a manner customarily reserved for terrorists. There is, in this circumstance, a grandiose irony, for the days are such that there are some terrorists in the land, even as there were in Rome when Peter wrote his letter; and the Berrigan brothers, who have proved redundantly that they are peaceful and nonviolent men, are among the very, very few to whom any American terrorists, or any of the now multitudes of youth tempted by the idea of terrorism as a means of social change, would listen. It is a measure of the illegitimacy of the State's action in America today that official violence would seek to capture and confine the very citizens who have an influence to deter or mitigate the unofficial violence in this land.

And so, what is a Christian who is a citizen to do?—elucidate and uphold the vocation of the emperor in a moment when that which is asserted and done in the name of the emperor is without legitimacy? The answer of the Berrigans —consistent, I suggest to you, with First Peter and with the scene of the early Church—is to *honor the emperor* by becoming a "fugitive from injustice," to become "powerless criminals in a day of criminal power."

> *But you are a chosen race, a royal priesthood, a holy nation, God's own people, that you may declare the wonderful deeds of him who called you out of darkness into his marvelous light. Once you were no people but now you are God's people; once you had not received mercy but now you have received mercy.*
>
> 1 Peter 2.9–10

The text in which the phrase *honor the emperor* appears affords another exegesis which affirms what has already been said, but which does so by giving due weight to the adjacent terms: *Honor all men. Love the brotherhood. Fear God.* Only, as it were, after all of these conditions are served does the matter arise of *honor the emperor*. Severally and jointly, these may, indeed, be taken as a description of the vocation of the emperor.

That alternative exegesis is not exhausted here, but I mention it because it does complement what has just been offered and because it is related directly to this other passage in the same letter concerning the Church and the people of the Church constituting a holy nation.

Furthermore, this passage about the Church is cited because I have no doubt that the most difficult burden the Berrigan brothers now suffer, in the federal prison at Danbury, is the condescension of those—still nominally free men—who remark that the Berrigans are prophets or martyrs and by that accusation attempt to dismiss their witness and evade the discomfiture it has brought to all who call themselves Christians in this country. One supposes the notion behind such pretenses is that the exercise of conscience—especially if at the peril of life or liberty—constitutes an individual eccentricity.

This letter of Peter—which is really a sermon on baptism—argues against any such quaint, solitary, unilateral, or private connotation of conscience. And the letter does so by placing the whole issue of *honor the emperor* in the middle of an exposition of the corporate integrity of the baptized community, of the Church of Christ as an exemplary nation, of the brotherhood of Christians as the precedent of mankind reconciled in society, of the Church living now in eschatological anticipation of the end and fulfillment of all (other) nations and societies, empires, authorities, regimes, presidencies, revolutions and assorted additional principalities and powers, of the Church of Christ, thus, standing always over against the emperor, rendering no more than suitable honor.

Daniel Berrigan and Philip Berrigan did not just personally conclude that the illegitimacy of the Vietnamese war is symptomatic of a more profound illegitimacy affecting both the officers and institutions of the State, but their witness—as in any use of conscience for a Christian—is as participants in the whole body of the Church, under the ecumenical discipline of baptism which makes them, as it does all Christians, responsible in a primary sense to all human beings.

The Berrigans have been the first to say that this does not imply that everyone else of the Church must imitate the specific Berrigan witness—any more than an equivalent consensus in action was characteristic among First Century Christians—but the reality of the Church in the issue of conscience does mean that every member of this body of Christ militant in this world—even in America—must now confront the same issue of illegitimacy in the State which the Berrigans have faced and, daily, are facing.

That is something, dear friends, which most of us have yet to do.

Or, as First Peter sums up the matter:

> *Baptism . . . now saves you, not as a removal of dirt from the body but as an appeal to God for a clear conscience, through the resurrection of Jesus Christ, who has gone into heaven and is at the right hand of God, with angels, authorities, and powers subject to him.*
>
> 1 Peter 3.21–22

III

CONSCIENCE, TACTICS, AND HOPE

Some days following Father Berrigan's unwanted departure
from Block Island, a telephone call was received from a prominent clergyman, the senior minister of a comfortable, rich,
white, Protestant congregation in that part of the country
which has come to be known as "middle America." The voice
on the phone seemed somehow excited—titillated, in fact—as
an invitation was conveyed to visit the congregation to speak
about "the crisis of conscience" which, it was presumed, we
had recently suffered in connection with Berrigan's visit to
our household. The message struck both of us, at the time,
as slightly morbid—this minister was, evidently, looking for
a dramatic entertainment for his congregants in which the
excruciation of deciding whether or not to receive Berrigan,
the criminal priest, would be related with suitable anguish.
Protestants in America have this notion that the exercise

of conscience is a form of self-torture—perhaps that partly explains how immobile and moribund conscience is in the churches.

The idea behind the proposal also impressed us as amusing, since neither of us had endured any epic of conscience regarding our friend Dan. The friendship amongst the three of us authorized—on the most straightforward and elementary human level—Dan to visit us whenever he wished to do so. At the time he became a fugitive, as has been indicated, it was mentioned casually that he might turn up at our home. There was no anguish or other anxiety involved in that brief conversation. Dan's peculiar legal status did not diminish our esteem for him and raised no issue about whether he would be welcome. There being nothing of substance to consider about that, it was not discussed.

Crisis of conscience, indeed! That clergyman on the telephone betrays an ignorance of what conscience is.

BAPTISM AND CONSCIENCE

This incident is not included here to ridicule the minister in question, but as an illustration of a widespread misapprehension of the meaning of conscience which exists within American society, and, most strangely and inappropriately, within the extant churches in the United States. It is a matter previously alluded to when criticism was made of those inclined to put down or evade the Berrigan witness by naming Daniel and Philip as prophets or martyrs, with the insinuation that they have indulged conscience idiosyncratically.

If conscience is no more than individualistic insight, void of social context, isolated from historical connections, without the discipline of human experience other than that of a single person, then we would argue that there is no such reality as conscience at all. We would, of course, allow any who like it to hold this view (though it seems to us manifestly nonsensical); our dispute is specifically with those who in such a fashion eliminate conscience so far as the Christian faith and community are concerned.

Conscience, in the Gospel, as well as in the actual experiences of the early Christians, refers to the new or restored maturity of human life in Christ. A person who becomes a Christian —speaking of that event in its biblical connotations as distinguished from any particular churchy traditions—suffers at once a personal and a public transfiguration. His insight into his own identity as a man is, at the same time, his acceptance of the rest of mankind. His reconciliation, that is, *his* experience of forgiveness, is profoundly private, but, simultaneously, his reconciliation is radically—even cosmically—political, incorporating *his* humanity into the whole of humanity, and, indeed, the whole of creating. If in religionizing Christianity and in domesticating the Church of Christ in America, many churchfolk have been deprived of this news of the political character of conversion, the truth remains unperturbed in the Bible, particularly in the evidence there of the style of life of the First Century Christians. The story of Ananias, who distrusted and dishonored this extraordinary covenant in Christ, and, at doing so "fell down and died," is one of the most striking citations, though there are many others.

Baptism, as practiced in the Apostolic Church, was the manner in which this corporate or political dimension of personal reconcilation was solemnized and publicized. The renewal of this man being baptized was understood to be relevant and good news for all men everywhere, not just for others of the Church. Each time a person was (is) baptized, the common life of all human beings in community was (is) affirmed and notarized.

The baptized man, thus, lives in a new, primary, and rudimentary relationship with other men signifying the reconciliation of the whole of life vouchsafed in Jesus Christ. The discernment—about any matter whatever—which is given and exercised in that remarkable relationship *is* conscience. In truth, the association of baptism with conscience, in this sense, is that conscience is properly deemed a charismatic gift.

Though to various other men, conscience may be a synonym for personal convenience, rationalization, eccentricity or even whim, as far as the Christian faith is concerned to deride or dismiss conscience in any such ways as these amounts to a denunciation of the Holy Spirit, a denial of its militancy, perhaps even a secret denial of its existence. To ignore or suppress conscience is to effectually gainsay the vitality of God's concern for human life in society here and now.

The inescapable issue in conscience for Christians is what has here been called the social or political context in which conscience is exercised; that social or political element in conscience refers concretely to the activity of the Holy Spirit historically upon the community of believers and the members of the community evoking their experience of renewed humanity for the sake and service of human life in the world. The initiative in conscience belongs to God; the authority of conscience is the maturity of the humanity of the Christian; the concern of conscience is always the societal fulfillment of life for all men. Still, the Christian community is diverse and dispersed, its members have different capabilities and locations, and the Holy Spirit is versatile, while the needs of the world, in the sense of humanizing life for mankind, are multifarious and cumulative and, not infrequently, contradictory. The exercise of conscience, therefore, is not the same thing as the arrival at consensus. In specific circumstances within a particular segment of the body of Christians, there may be a coincidence of conscience and consensus, but there may also be conscientious fitness not attended by consensus or there may even be many simultaneous voices of conscience, some of which seem inconsistent one with another. That conscience is not mechanical or narrow but free in its use and far-reaching we take to be a tribute to the vigor and versatility of the Holy

Spirit, as well as a sign of the imagination and seriousness with which Christians are called to regard and become involved in history.

Pietists, among them some partisans of natural law, will complain that this comprehension of functioning conscience within the Christian witness makes evaluation of any particular action, which is said to be conscientious, difficult. That we readily concede; it is, in fact, impossible, and we gladly recall that the prerogative of judgment of conscience is vested in God, not in men, not in laws, not in the State, not in the ethics of culture, not in the Church, and certainly not in the churches, sects, and denominations. What transpires, in decisions and actions of conscience, on the part of a Christian or of some community of Christians or of many Christians positioned diversely, is a living encounter between the Holy Spirit and those deciding and acting in relation to human needs in society. If either those who act or those who stand apart from the action presume judgment of what is said and done they negate the viability of that encounter. The practice of conscience, thus, is an extraordinarily audacious undertaking, disdaining all mundane or conventional prudential calculations and confessing the exclusivity of God's judgment and trusting God's judgment as grace. Conscience requires knowing and respecting one's self as no less, but no more, than human. The exercise of conscience represents—as First Peter remarks—living as a free man.

How, in historic actual circumstances, conscience may err remains, mercifully, God's secret insight, but that conscience may err becomes no excuse for any default, abstention, or silence, or for any substitution of prudence for conscience, since none of these common recourses are spared God's judgment either, though each of them exposes those who would retreat into them as men who are not free as human beings and who are very impudent toward God.

To ease the issue of God's judgment, or to feign to evade

God's judgment, many construe the use of conscience as an abstract and *a priori* problem and, hence, indulge, often ingeniously in hypothetical speculations about what decision should be had in imagined situations. They seek, we suppose, in this manner to anticipate contingencies and prepare in advance to meet them and, we suspect, hope to reduce the trauma of decision-making and, as it were, minimize the pertinence of judgment. Yet conscience, at least in its Christian form, is *never* a hypothetical game, and to turn into such an indulgence both abuses history by taking persons and events less seriously than in their actuality and devalues the judgment of God, which always concerns and addresses that which is historically concrete.

Thus, after Berrigan's presence in our home while a fugitive, we have been frequently asked if we would receive other fugitives—Angela Davis? Timothy Leary? a Quebec terrorist? a draft dodger?—to which we have replied that we do not know what we would decide to do if confronted with any such questions. We await, in conscientious decisions, the real situation. We welcomed Dan. The controlling circumstances in that action did not happen in August of 1970, but long before, in 1964, when Berrigan and Towne and Stringfellow first met and became friends. Just so is every conscientious act historic, in living context, serious, free of advance restriction or hypothetical commitment, and wholly vulnerable to God's judgment.

CONSCIENCE AND RESISTANCE

Assuming that the word inspiration can be used without its sentimental or indefinite connotations, we would say that conscience involves a conjunction of inspiration with common life or, put theologically, conscience is the access of the Holy Spirit to human beings in their decisions and actions in daily existence. That the Holy Spirit is implicated with conscientious deliberation, that inspiration can inform thought and deed does not imply that conscience is irrational, antirational, or nonrational; on the contrary, conscience, by taking actuality soberly, engages reason in a notably mature way.

The contemporary American scene is one in which it seems exeptional to be rational, much less to discipline reason in conscience. That is variously and amply manifest, on several levels of society, but nowhere is it more evident than in the currency of American babel. Words, in their public usage, have become so abused that they seldom relate to factual truth. Both of us, one as a poet and the other as a lawyer, are, perhaps, especially sensitive to language; both of us are convinced that the meaning of words should have integrity in reality and that words should be employed with veracity and straightforwardness. Alas, an extraordinary distortion of language has been taking place over the past several years—coincident, significantly, with the demise of the civil rights movement, the fatigue wrought by war, a public acquiescence to official deception or, as it is called, "the credibility gap," and a greatly increased construction of politics as a subdivision of public relations. This verbal debilitation has by now reached a point where very many public words and phrases have been inverted in meaning and/or are utilized with the most contemptuous disregard of the truth in a factual sense. Public language is always stylized and ritualistic, but American public language has become corrupted by code words, gross euphemisms, and phoniness.

An example at hand, as this is being written, is found in a political campaign in which the President of the United States —to mention no others, though some have succumbed to even greater irrational excesses—has repeatedly condemned candidates "who condone violence." Factually, the truth is that there are no such candidates anywhere in sight. Nevertheless, the

President as campaigner is unhesitant about imputing the approval or advocacy of violence to those he nominates as his opponents because, among other things, violence as a term has acquired such inexact and, indeed, inverse associations in the public mind. One recalls, in the mid-sixties, when the word "violence" and other words of violent sound—like "riot" or "crime-in-the-streets"—began to be (mis)applied, deliberately to the *nonviolent* civil rights demonstrations and then to the early *peaceful* antiwar marches. This was typical of Deep Southern racists and standard doctrine in the John Birch Society, but it was also a deception perpetrated in the Goldwater presidential bid; it has become incorporated into the official rhetoric of the police in many jurisdictions; it has found eager acceptance and repetition among those whose status has been chiefly challenged by social protest—among the middle-aged white bourgeoisie. The false connection of peaceful dissent and nonviolent protest with violence, the guilty association of "riot" or "crime" with "demonstration" or "march," has virtually succeeded in equating advocacy of significant social change with terrorism or, as has been witnessed, in the example of the President, in fantastically construing opposition to Nixon as condonation of violence. For white middle-class Americans, we fear, the redundant separation of words from their truthful meaning and context, the inversion of public language, the abusive application of terms and phrases despite facts to the contrary has prompted such an incoherence that now a whole disparate array of acts, symbols, words, gestures—that is, long hair, obscenity, rock music, the hippie style, together with demonstrations, dissidence, complaint, and protest—are all jumbled together, in one large bag, conveying an impression of violence whether or not, in any specific circumstances, violence of any order is intended or has taken place.

The extent of the babel in America at the present time was symbolized for us on the Sunday following Dan Berrigan's

capture. Some of the Islanders and some of the summer
people, on their own initiative, organized a "Dan Berrigan
Day" on Block Island. Their idea was to both better acquaint
their neighbors and visitors with Berrigan, with his thoughts
and with his action, and to express gratitude for his witness.
Posters bearing excerpts from some of Dan's poems and books
were prepared and put around the village. A mimeographed
sheet, presenting a brief biography and a few Berrigan quota-
tions, was circulated at the docks where the ferries arrive. A
gathering was held at which some readings from Berrigan's
books were heard. There was, to our knowledge, only one
public gesture of hostility toward Dan displayed that day.
A summer resident carried a sign back and forth in the
vicinity of the Dan Berrigan Day observances; its legend read,
"Priest Preaches Violence." While neither of us spoke with
the man carrying this sign, we are told by several people who
did talk with him that efforts to point out the falsity of his
impression of what this priest preaches were of no avail, for
in his mind the sign man was convinced that *any* protest
means violence.

White middle-class Americans, like this picket, suffer such
obstinate confusion partly because they *want* to believe that
all opposition to the status quo is violent so that repression,
suppression, punishment, or violent reprisal can apparently be
justified. This conclusion becomes convincing when one beholds—for a single example of the many that might be cited—
the indictments handed up, after the Scranton Commission
findings critical of the National Guard conduct at Kent State
University, against students and faculty who were the most
influential in advocating and practicing peaceful tactics prior
to and following the Kent State massacre. The conclusion becomes inescapable when one reads the FBI report which
factually refutes the basis of the indictments and vindicates
the Scranton findings.

Perchance something like the Hobart or the Kent State

indictments furnishes a clue to the more profound issues of
social pathology which underlie the manipulation of language
by the President and by others aping his ethics and skills.
Perhaps this incredible inversion of words—notably where it
pertains to violence—is possibly only as a calculated and cruel
exploitation of the sense of guilt which afflicts and entraps
white Americans and so paralyzes their human faculties that
they become eager to embrace any scapegoat, any lie, any fake
expiation, any contention that shifts the blame.

The babel spreads in many directions; the confusion is pervasive. Another aspect of it, closely related to the issue of
violence, concerns the so-called underground. In a season when
scapegoats are being officially promoted, for the diversion of
the majority classes, the notion circulates that there exists
a revolutionary conspiracy, aiming at anarchy and practicing
terrorism, with a sophisticated, clandestine organization. We
do not know whether such exists or not, but we realize that
the allusion is not to the Mafia (which seems still to flourish
without significant governmental interference) but to a very
motley array of rebels, resisters, dissidents and nonconformists.
Spasmodic bombings of banks and public buildings evidence
that there are some few terrorists at large, but an issue arises
when these happenings become linked in public mind with the
wide variety of nonterrorist citizens in protest and resistance,
so that a monolithic, indiscriminate image is concocted and
applied to all dissenters and rebels. To lump together those
who have engaged in sabotage with those who utter Anglo-
Saxon obscenities as "thugs" plaguing "the good people"—as
the President, in a performance stridently reminiscent of the
very earliest of his several political incarnations, has repeatedly
done—is both calculated dishonesty and willfully provocative.

At the same time, those in assorted postures of social protest have sown confusion, too, by employing the nomenclature
of an "underground" to designate—and, maybe, to romanticize

—multifarious actions ranging from burning draft cards to wearing fragments of Old Glory on the seat of the pants, to flight to Sweden or Canada or elsewhere, to sit-ins and building seizures, to the withholding of taxes, to the unauthorized celebration of the eucharist. Any of these, and similar, efforts may be obnoxious to authority, or, in specific circumstances, some may be illegal, but none are, in principle, violent, and all are a very far cry from anarchism or revolutionary terrorism. We think it has seriously aggravated the social panic in America to denominate such disparate actions under the same rubric as that of any terrorists that may be around.

In the Berrigan case, any number of persons had contact and conversation with the fugitive, and sometimes Dan's elusion of the FBI was described by journalists as an "underground" existence. On occasion, as in the homily in the preface to this book, Berrigan himself invoked the name "underground" as a way of explicating his situation biblically.

So the confusion is a fact. Mindful of somewhat similar circumstances predecessor Christians encountered during the First Century, in seeking to distinguish their witness from that of idolators of the State, on one hand, and from the zealotic revolutionaries, on the other, we do not suppose that it can be dispelled. And we have no exception that the public authorities—particularly considering their current readiness to interpret the conspiracy laws (which are of the most dubious constitutional status) so loosely—will be any more comprehending for a Christian political witness in the U.S.A. than in imperial Rome, especially where the witness compels Christians to confront substantive issues like those affecting the legitimacy of the State and the tactics of revolutionary change in society.

It is a bad scene that is symbolized by this babel in which violence can be falsely imputed to any protest, or in which the pathological anxieties of the white majority can be politically manipulated and managed in order to license repression, or in which the police have so far been captivated by a conspiratorial mentality that illegal surveillance, the use of informers and contempt for constitutional rights become commonplace and even elicit popular support, or in which capricious indictments and political prosecutions corrupt due process of law. It is pathetically ironic too, for where nonviolent protest is treated as equivalent to terrorism, it nourishes a cynicism about the prospects for any significant social change and drastically alters the tactical options available to those who seek such change. To discredit nonviolence by ridiculing or suppressing it, as if it were violence, becomes persuasive—to many—that violence is the only means by which protest can be heard, the only way change can be accomplished, and, failing that, at least the resort through which the status quo will suffer harassment, disruption, and an accelerated disintegration.

That represents a familiar irony, since it is reminiscent of what happened in the early sixties in the black revolt. For nearly a decade, the American black rebellion had been dominated by the ethics and tactics of nonviolence, exemplified —incarnated, really—in Martin Luther King. That unprecedented witness of the potency and efficacy of peaceful protest, sustained for ten fateful years, was met, consistently, in both Northern cities and Southern hinterlands, by white violence, often under a claim of legality, abetted by the apathy and default of the white majority. The intransigence of whites toward black nonviolence prompted a challenge from within the black community to tactical nonviolence. Violence, it was argued, was the only ethic that whites understood, the only one they practiced, the means they glorified and, thus, was the only recourse to which whites could be expected to pay attention and, perhaps, respond in terms of social change. Well, white violence thus brought black nonviolence to an end, for a while at least, and white violence perversely inspired black violence, which erupted in riots in hundreds of cities, but that, in turn, has wrought no significant racial change in society; it has only occasioned repression and death and the mobilization and deployment of an overwhelming, militarized, white counterviolence enforcing the American apartheid. The riots have been quashed, the black ghettos live under siege, the white ghettos have a form of martial law, and the prospects for change are drastically diminished. White violence still prevails.

As if to regurgitate this history, where there has been campus unrest, discontent among the young and antiwar protests, official violence and the impugning of peaceful tactics as if they constituted violence, along with the pursuit of those who uphold nonviolence as if they were terrorists, there has been once more an estopping of nonviolence as a route to social change and a luring of many rebels, notably among the young, into violence as, apparently, the only resort to which established authority harkens.

What emerges from this situation, particularly among white youth, is a violence of despair: a tactics of disruption, destruction, and waste, bereft of expectation of serious change in society or of human promise for a viable future, and thus a fixation upon little more than a transient relief from frustration, or the enactment of outrage and defiance. In this way, the purpose of death—so ascendant, so pervasive, so relentless, so insatiable in the American status quo—assumes another guise, no less aggressive and dehumanizing, to capture the erstwhile revolutionaries.

Can nothing be done to alter the demoralized atmosphere in which young and old, black and white, rebellious and conformed exist? Could not some change in the temperament of these days be brought to pass that could signify hope or, at the least, provide counterpoint to the despair and anger that makes so many citizens the foes of one another? Is there no gesture available to government that could mute or mitigate the coercion of the State enough to elicit respect from a larger constituency? Is there no way to refute violence in this land?

We think there be some steps which, if undertaken sincerely and urgently, could do much to dispel the reign of death which, at once, entraps officialdom and those beholden to the status quo as well as professed revolutionaries. A signal, for example, could be the extension of amnesty to war resisters and other dissidents who have been in exile or in prison. We have in mind an array of citizens whose circumstances—as draft objectors, deserters from the military services, and those whose opposition to war has entailed technically illegal acts and who have been imprisoned for such political action—warrant amnesty, either in accordance with precedents for amnesty in America's history (in the Reconstruction era or after the world wars, for example) or, in any case, according to society's present, pathetic need to interrupt the cycle of official and unofficial violence which threatens to encompass and destroy, in one way or another, everyone. Assorted war resisters do not exhaust the roster. There are, as well, black citizens who are prisoners of conscience and whose cases involve abuses of due process that cannot be overlooked for the sake of a social future for the country, just as much as for their behalf.

We can foresee both a general amnesty for exiles and deserters and a judicially convened extraordinary tribunal to review the case of any prisoner—on petition of the prisoner or, conceivably, public intercessors—whose conviction can be shown to be significantly related to political protest or conscientious action. There are Americans, we are aware, so narrow in their comprehension of politics, so apprehensive of social change, so insecure in their construction of citizenship, and, most of all, so obtuse to the societal debilitation wrought by coercion, repression, and violence in these last years that they would conceive such amnesty remedies to be too exceptional. They see only a need for more efficient repression. To such fellow citizens, we suggest that the course they favor is suicidal and we emphasize that a general amnesty for war resisters and a nonpolitical tribunal to examine the situations of prisoners of conscience and asserted political prisoners do not constitute very radical, generous, or gratuitous measures. In themselves they would not reconcile this society. But in themselves they would challenge the rule of violence, they would extend a tentative hope, they might be therapeutic insofar as they symbolized new or different means for this society to cope with dissidence and protest.

Meanwhile, where the ethics of change condone or practice violence, then revolution—no matter how idealistic, how necessary, or how seemingly glorious—is basically without viable hope even if it were to prevail empirically. And where the tactics of protest practice violence, but where expectation of change has been defeated, then despair reigns. In such circumstances, though we are not ideological pacifists—or, for that matter, ideologues of any species, we are persuaded, as are the Berrigans, that recourse to violence, whether to threaten or topple the idol of death in the State, is inherently a worship of the self-same idol.

And so we persevere, as Christians, and, simply, as human beings, in nonviolence. We do so whether or not the witness is understood or distinguished as such by the political authorities, and whether or not any revolutionaries advocating violence count it effective. We do so because nonviolence has become the *only* way in America, today, to express hope for human life in society, and, transcending that, to anticipate an eschatological hope.

A COMMON JEOPARDY: A COMMON HOPE

One of the ironies of our present situation is that everyone —those who are against us as much as those who are for us— assumes that we did something for Daniel Berrigan. We did, gladly, give our hospitality to him, of course, as we have on many other occasions. Still, in this visit, the more significant fact is that Dan did something for us.

Those who followed his interviews and articles and other messages during the months he remained at liberty as a fugitive know that Father Berrigan put increasing emphasis upon the necessity of extemporizing new modes of living as community in America even as the inherited social order— including the churchly institutions—is being exposed as anti-human and becomes manifestly desperate.

Berrigan's witness, though fixed upon Vietnam as the grue-some epitomy of death, as a moral power, ruling the nation and literally demoralizing its citizens, transcends the war. While being hunted as if he were a criminal, Berrigan has been expounding, exemplifying, nurturing life: Berrigan has been showing us, and all of us, a more excellent way, as it has pre-viously been named, in which life is constantly being emanci-pated from death, in which human beings are not awed or cowered by the State, in which there is a hope for a society worthy of human life.

We have no doubt that Dan perseveres in this same task from within the federal penitentiary at Danbury. Indeed, we intuit that his fugitive status during the past four months and his fate now as a captive, if not essential to such a ministry today in America, at the least is a seal of its authenticity and of its authority.

And of its appeal. Daniel Berrigan has not been engaged in a solitary or eccentric witness, but one with which *so* many other persons have identified—from the virtually anonymous ranks of those who have, like Dan and like his brother Philip, suffered prosecution and imprisonments for political reasons, to those who have been driven by conscience into exile from their birthright, to still more, like ourselves— that, in truth, an astonishing ecumenical community has been called into being. It is, we suppose, too much to expect official comprehension of this reality by the authorities of the State, or by others imbued with a conspiratorial mentality, or, for that matter, by any pharisees, or by very many of the hierarchs. Nevertheless, there it is—Father Berrigan has been, and remains, in our midst improvising the Church.

All of this is related, obviously, to the specific jeopardy which Berrigan has borne as a defendant, as a convicted felon, as a fugitive, and which he now bears, in solidarity with so many others, as a prisoner. Yet the jeopardy does not attach to him alone, as he knows, and he has not been and is not alone in bearing it. His particular jeopardy symbolizes and represents —it, practically speaking, sacramentalizes—a common jeopardy threatening all citizens who do not conform, who will not lapse into silence, who refuse to acquiesce to the totalitarianization of the nation, and who, thus, decline to resign as human beings.

"A community of resistance" it has been called. Father Berrigan baptized it "a community of risk." Some speak of it as an emergent "confessing movement," in that way invoking a previous experience of Christians and others in the days of the Nazi totalitarianism. We are ready to testify that there is, in America, now, a community of resurrection, sharing a common jeopardy—death—in order to live in a common hope as human beings.

IV

DOCUMENTS OF THE
BLOCK ISLAND CASE

Much of this book was written prior to the authors' indictment in December 1970. All of the legal documents, together with related statements of the defendants and of their defense committee, and the opinion of the court discussing the indictment, are here reproduced in full.

The documents are included—rather than reducing the Block Island case to a narrative—for a variety of reasons. One is to furnish the story of the case in the least subjective way. Another is to inform readers of the scope of effort, legal and otherwise, required in even a relatively straightforward case. A third reason is to explicate the issues of the Block Island case.

These papers cannot be published without expressing the appreciation which the authors have for Edwin Hastings, Esq., of Providence, R.I., their chief defense counsel, and for his associates in the case.

Indictment No. 7709

IN THE DISTRICT COURT OF THE UNITED STATES
FOR THE DISTRICT OF RHODE ISLAND

UNITED STATES OF AMERICA
v.
WILLIAM STRINGFELLOW and
ANTHONY TOWNE

Indictment No. 7709
Vio. Title 18, U.S.C., Sections
1071 and 3

The Grand Jury charges:

Count 1

That from on or about August 7, 1970, the exact date being unknown to the Grand Jury, up to and including on or about

August 11, 1970, at New Shoreham, commonly known as Block Island, in the District of Rhode Island WILLIAM STRING-FELLOW and ANTHONY TOWNE did unlawfully, willfully, and knowingly harbor and conceal Daniel Berrigan so as to prevent the discovery and arrest of the said Daniel Berrigan, for whose arrest a warrant had been issued under the provisions of a law of the United States by the United States District Court for the District of Maryland on April 9, 1970, after his conviction in that Court of destruction of government property and wilful interference with the administration of the Military Selective Service Act (18 U.S.C. 1361 and 2071 and 50 Appx. U.S.C. 462 (a)), and who had failed to surrender himself at the direction of the Court to commence service of the sentence imposed upon him, the said WILLIAM STRINGFELLOW and ANTHONY TOWNE well knowing that the said warrant and process had been issued for the apprehension of the said Daniel Berrigan, as aforesaid; in violation of Title 18, United States Code, Section 1071.

Count 2

The Grand Jury further charges:

That from on or about August 7, 1970, the exact date being unknown to the Grand Jury, up to and including on or about August 11, 1970, at New Shoreham, commonly known as Block Island, in the District of Rhode Island, WILLIAM STRING-FELLOW and ANTHONY TOWNE, knowing that Daniel Berrigan had committed offenses against the United States, that is, destruction of government property and wilful interference with the administration of the Military Selective Service Act (18 U.S.C. 1361 and 2017 and 50 Appx. U.S.C. 462(a)), in the District of Maryland, did unlawfully, wilfully, and knowingly relieve, receive, comfort and assist the said Daniel Berrigan in order to prevent and hinder his punishment, that is to say,

WILLIAM STRINGFELLOW and ANTHONY TOWNE, well knowing the facts as aforesaid, did receive Daniel Berrigan in their residence on New Shoreham, commonly called Block Island, and there did offer and give sustenance and lodging to him; in violation of Title 18, United States Code, Section 3.

A TRUE BILL

ALBERT E. MITCHELL
Foreman

LINCOLN C. ALMOND
United States Attorney

A Statement by the Accused

A STATEMENT BY ANTHONY TOWNE AND WILLIAM STRINGFELLOW OF BLOCK ISLAND, R.I., CONCERNING INDICTMENT NUMBER 7709 IN THE UNITED STATES DISTRICT COURT FOR RHODE ISLAND.

Grave charges have been made against us by the public authorities and we have pleaded innocent to those charges because we *are* innocent. In due course, a jury of our fellow citizens will have an opportunity to uphold our innocence and we await their verdict with cheerful expectations.

Daniel Berrigan is our friend. We rejoice in that fact and strive to be worthy of it. Our hospitality to Daniel Berrigan is no crime. At a certain time and in a certain place we did "relieve, receive, comfort and assist" him and we did "offer and give sustenance and lodging" to him. We did not "harbor" or "conceal" him. We did not "hinder" the authorities.

Father Berrigan has and had no need to be concealed. By his own extraordinary vocation, and by the grace of God, he has become one of the conspicuous Christians of these wretched times. We have done what we could do to affirm him in this regard. We categorically deny that we have done anything to conceal him.

We are not disposed to hide what light there is under a bushel.

Our indictment has not happened in a void. We cannot ignore the scene in which such a remarkable event takes place: the manifold and multiplying violence of this society, the alienation between races and generations, the moral fatigue of Americans, the debilitating atmosphere in which citizens become so suspicious and fearful of their own government that they suppose silence is the only safety and conformity the only way to survive.

Because we are innocent, we believe that we would not have been indicted but for the pervasiveness of the spirit of repression which has lately overtaken the nation.

In that respect, we consider that whatever happens to us will in truth be happening to all Americans.

And so, to our fellow citizens, we say:

The violence must end.

All violence must stop.

The vainglorious war in Asia must cease now, but more than that, the war enterprise must be dismantled and the military predominance in our society must be reversed.

And the violence of political terrorists must end now. Arson, kidnapping, bombing in fact sabotage the social change the nation so pathetically needs, and such tactics are just as wrong and just as futile as the violence of war and racism and repression.

The psychological violence, sometimes officially condoned, by which citizens are accused and impugned without opportunity for appropriate reply and are otherwise harassed, spied upon, frightened or intimidated must be stopped now.

These are all works of death. Only when our country is free of them will it be a society in which men can rejoice as human beings.

We make this statement as our Christmas greeting—especially to Daniel and Philip Berrigan, to all prisoners of conscience, and to all Americans who wish to be free.

A Statement by the Committee for the Defense of William Stringfellow and Anthony Towne

We have gathered for the defense of William Stringfellow and Anthony Towne who, shortly before Christmas, 1970, were indicted for allegedly "harboring and concealing" Daniel Berrigan, S.J., a fugitive, and for allegedly hindering punishment of Father Berrigan for an offense of which he had been convicted by relieving, receiving, comforting, assisting, and giving sustenance and lodging to him.

The accused have pleaded innocent to these charges and have stated that their friendship and hospitality for Father Berrigan is no crime. They believe they would not have been indicted but for a pervasive spirit of repression in America.

Among us there are various reasons for joining this effort to ensure Towne and Stringfellow an effective defense and the funds and other resources necessary for it:

1) Most of us know the accused personally as men of decency, conscience, and compassion who have often helped others and who now need help themselves.

2) From their books and public witness we recognize the defendants as citizens with creative and courageous ideas, whose social criticism—especially when it is controversial—is indispensable if society is to be free. We all applaud their consistent espousal and practice of non-violence in social protest.

3) Many of us are primarily concerned for peace, both overseas and at home. There would be no prosecutions such as this but for the moral attrition America has suffered in the past decade on account of the war in Viet Nam which has furnished a political context for this proceeding, affecting the freedom of all citizens and not of the accused alone.

4) Some of us believe this case may assume an unexpectedly large importance in American life in the disposition of conflicts between conscientious actions and the authority of the State and, in turn, of constitutional issues respecting the free practice of religion.

We purpose not only to render moral and practical support, but also to be closely attentive to the prosecution and trial of William Stringfellow and Anthony Towne. We urge and invite our fellow citizens to join us in doing the same.

DR. JOHN C. BENNETT
Chairman

REV. MELVIN E. SCHOONOVER
National Coordinator

Defendants' Motion to Dismiss Count I

UNITED STATES DISTRICT COURT

FOR THE

DISTRICT OF RHODE ISLAND

UNITED STATES OF AMERICA

v.

WILLIAM STRINGFELLOW and

ANTHONY TOWNE

Indictment No. 7709

Motion to Dismiss

Defendants respectfully move that Count I of the Indictment for alleged violation of 18 U.S.C. §1071 ("Concealing person from arrest") be dismissed on the following grounds:

(1) Count I of the indictment is defective under Rule 7(c) of the Federal Rules of Criminal Procedure in that it does not state the essential facts constituting the offense charged.

(2) Count I of the indictment is defective under Article V of Amendments to the Constitution of the United States in that it is not specific enough to insure that it is the indictment of the Grand Jury rather than the indictment of the prosecutor.

(3) Count I of the indictment is defective under Article VI of Amendments to the Constitution of the United States in that it does not with reasonable certainty apprise the defendants with the nature of the accusation against them.

(4) Count I of the indictment is defective in that it uses only the language of the statute and is not accompanied by such a statement of the facts and circumstances as will inform the defendants of the specific offense with which they are charged.

By their attorneys,

EDWIN H. HASTINGS
DEWITTE T. KERSH, JR.

Tillinghast, Collins & Graham
1030 Hospital Trust Building
Providence, Rhode Island 02903
(401-274-3800)

To Lincoln B. Almond, Esq.

U.S. Attorney

Please take notice that the undersigned will bring the above motion on for hearing before the United States Court for the District of Rhode Island on February 1, 1971, at 10:00 A.M. or as soon thereafter as counsel can be heard.

EDWIN H. HASTINGS

Certificate of Service

I certify that on January 5, 1971, I served a copy of this foregoing motion upon Lincoln B. Almond, Esq., by delivery to his office.

EDWIN H. HASTINGS

Memorandum of Law

UNITED STATES DISTRICT COURT

FOR THE

DISTRICT OF RHODE ISLAND

UNITED STATES OF AMERICA

v.

WILLIAM STRINGFELLOW and

ANTHONY TOWNE

Indictment No. 7709

Memorandum in Support of Defendants' Motion to Dismiss Count I of the Indictment

Rule 7(c) of the Federal Rules of Criminal Procedure requires that the indictment state "the essential facts constituting the offense charged." Count I of the indictment states no facts other than the statutory language. Count II, by contrast, does state specific facts alleged to constitute a violation of another statute.

Under the leading case relating to the sufficiency of indictments, *Russell* v. *United States*, 369 U.S. 749 (1962), the court, in an extensive opinion by Mr. Justice Stewart, discussed rule 7(c) in the light of the Fifth and Sixth Amendments at pages 760–766 and held defective an indictment which did not sufficiently apprise a defendant of what he must be prepared to meet.

Among other things the court stated (369 U.S. at 765–766) (quoting with approval from earlier Supreme Court decisions):

> It is an elementary principle of criminal pleading, that where the definition of an offence, whether it be at common law or by statute, "includes generic terms, it is not sufficient that the indictment shall charge the offence in the same generic terms as in the definition; but it must state the species—it must descend to particulars." [citation] An indictment not framed to apprise the defendant "with reasonable certainty, of the nature of the accusation against him . . . is defective, although it may follow the language of the statute." [citation] "In an indictment upon a statute, it is not sufficient to set forth the offence in the words of the statute, unless those words of themselves fully, directly, and expressly, without any uncertainty or ambiguity, set forth all the elements necessary to constitute the offence intended to be punished . . ." [citation] "Undoubtedly the language of the statute may be used in the general description of an offence, but it must be accompanied with such a statement of the facts and circumstances as will inform the accused of the specific offence, coming under the general description, with which he is charged." [citations] That these basic principles of fundamental fairness retain their full vitality under modern concepts of pleading, and specifically under Rule 7(c) of the Federal Rules of Criminal Procedure, is illustrated by many recent federal decisions.

The court went on to state that the purpose of the requirement of facts sufficiently specific was, among other things, to "enable the court to decide whether the facts alleged are sufficient in law to withstand a motion to dismiss the indictment or to support a conviction in the event that one should be had" (369 U.S. at page 768, note 15 and discussion pages 768–769).

As to the function of the indictment and the grand jury, the court went on to say at 369 U.S. at page 370:

> A grand jury, in order to make that ultimate determination [as to whether a person should be held to answer in a criminal trial] must necessarily determine what the question under inquiry was. To allow the prosecutor, or the court, to make a subsequent guess as to what was in the minds of the grand jury at the time they returned the indictment would deprive the defendant of a basic protection which the guaranty of the intervention of a grand jury was designed to secure. For a defendant could then be convicted on the basis of facts not found by, and perhaps not even presented to, the grand jury which indicted him.

Applying the teachings of *Russell* v. *United States* to Count I of the instant indictment, the principal question before the grand jury under 18 U.S.C. §1071 was whether the acts said to have been committed by defendants amounted to secreting a person alleged to be subject to an arrest warrant.

The leading cases on harboring and concealing, *Firpo* v. *United States,* 261 Fed. 850 (2d Cir. 1919) (Manton, J.), and *United States* v. *Shapiro*, 113 F.2d 891 (2nd Cir. 1940) (Swan, J.) both make it clear that "harboring and concealing" refer "to some physical act tending to the secretion of the body of the offender."

No such physical acts are alleged in Count I of the indictment. Count II of the indictment alleges that certain acts were performed by defendants—namely the giving of "sustenance and lodging," which acts would appear to a reader of Webster not to involve "secretion of the body of the offender."

Accordingly, we respectfully submit that inasmuch as Count I of the indictment charges the defendants with no specific acts (such as were charged and found to be insufficient in *Shapiro* and in *Firpo, supra*) which tend to the secretion of the body of the offender, and said Count I is generally insufficient to apprise defendants of what they must be prepared to meet, as well as insufficient to illuminate what was in the minds of the grand jury or to enable the courts—trial or appellate—to determine whether an indictment or conviction may stand, Count I should be dismissed.

Respectfully submitted,
By their attorneys,

EDWIN H. HASTINGS
DeWITTE T. KERSH, JR.

Tillinghast, Collins & Graham
1030 Hospital Trust Building
Providence, Rhode Island 02903
(401–274–3800)

Supplemental Memorandum

UNITED STATES DISTRICT COURT
FOR THE
DISTRICT OF RHODE ISLAND

UNITED STATES OF AMERICA
v.
WILLIAM STRINGFELLOW and
ANTHONY TOWNE

Indictment No. 7709

Supplemental Memorandum of Defendants
in Regard to Motion to Dismiss Count I

In our earlier memorandum, we discussed at some length *Russell* v. *United States,* 369 U.S. 749 (1962) as applied to Count I of the indictment, which is a "bare-bones" indictment setting forth no facts other than generalized allegations in the language of the statute (28 U.S.C. §1071).

The instant case is an unusual one, not a common type of "crime" with which the court is frequently faced (tax evasion, anti-trust, rape, robbery, etc.), and it may be helpful to the court, in its analysis of the sufficiency of Count I, to consider the Count, not only in the light of *Russell,* but in the light of some additional cases, one of which raises some considerations paralleling some of those involved herein, *Van Liew* v. *United States,* 321 F.2d 664 (5th Cir. 1963), and another of which is an important indictment decision of this Court, *United States* v. *Apex Distributing Co.,* 148 F. Supp. 365 (D.R.I. 1957).

Turning first to *Van Liew,* it involved charges of adulterating and misbranding orange juice. The product labeled "orange juice" was an orange drink made of orange juice and certain additives. The government conceded that the orange drink was pure and wholesome and had as many vitamins as freshly-squeezed orange juice.

An indictment following statutory language was held defective, and the court, discussing *Russell* and other cases, made, among others, the following points which the Court in the instant case may consider relevant:

(1) The obvious point that the offense must be set forth with clearness and all necessary certainty for the information of the accused;

(2) A less obvious point described by the Court in *Van Liew* at page 669:

> the presentment by a Grand Jury has in our constitutional scheme another basic function. It is the protection to the citizen against unfounded charges. Little may be left open to construction or interpretation of an indictment. If the offense is not plainly stated and is made so only by a process of interpretation, there is no assurance that the Grand Jury would have charged such an offense.

(3) The special need for an adequate statement of facts and circumstances to be set forth where severe penalties of fine and imprisonment may be exacted for the commission of acts which are generally regarded as at worst innocuous or at best commendable.

Thus in *Van Liew* at page 674:

> When, as this statute permits, innocuous and morally innocent
> actions may send men to jail for long periods of time because
> mistakes in processing or labeling, etc., result in "economic"
> adulteration, it is essential that the offense (or offenses) be
> identified and charged in terms which adequately relate the
> actions to the statute.

We respectfully suggest that *Russell* and *Van Liew* have
unusual pertinency to Count I of the instant indictment. We
have a situation where Count I alleges no specific overt acts
at all, and Count II alleges only that defendants gave "sustenance and lodging" to another person.

Such acts (if they are the overt acts with which Count I is
concerned) are even more "innocuous and morally innocent"
than misbranding or adulteration of orange juice, and defendants should be entitled to as much specificity in Count I
as they are accorded in Count II.

Possibly, the key question in the light of *Van Liew* and
Russell, however, is whether the "Grand Jury would have
charged such an offense" had the indictment itself informed
the Grand Jury of the overt acts which in the opinion of the
United States Attorney comprised the offenses of "harboring
and concealing." Is there enough in the indictment for the
Court itself to tell upon what facts the Grand Jury relied, or
whether such facts if proven would constitute the crime as
a matter of law.

Directly bearing on these questions is the 1957 decision of
this Court, *United States* v. *Apex Distributing Co.,* 148 F.
Supp. 365, which antedated but foreshadowed *Russell,* and
which was one of several district and circuit decisions relied
upon in *Russell* (369 U.S. 749 at 766, n. 13). Another of the
cases relied upon in *Russell* was a Massachusetts decision which
in turn had relied upon and followed *Apex* [*United States* v.
Devine's Milk Laboratories, 179 F. Supp. 799 (1960), Ford, J.].

In *Apex,* this Court dismissed Part B of Count I and Counts

IV, V, VI and VII in a case involving charges of defrauding the United States and bribing a naval officer, saying, among other things, at page 370:

> While it is true that where the object of a conspiracy is to commit a crime, the crime to be committed need not be described with the same degree of particularity that might be required in an indictment charging its commission as a substantive offense, *this does not mean that no particulars whatever as to such crime need be given. And this is especially true where the statute employs broad and comprehensive language descriptive of the general nature of the offense denounced.* [Emphasis added]

As to omissions of particulars from Counts IV and V, the court refused to accept statutory language in the indictment as sufficient, saying at page 372:

> In each of said counts there is merely the allegation that the defendants "did make and present . . . a false, fictitious and fraudulent claim upon and against the United States, said defendants then and there knowing such claim to be false, fictitious and fraudulent." In neither of them is there any description or identification of said false, fictitious or fraudulent claim; nor is there any statement of the particular or particulars wherein said claim was false, fictitious and fraudulent. In my opinion, the omission of allegations as to these essential facts is fatal.

Looking to the three essential tests in *Russell, Van Liew* and *Apex Distributing,* can it fairly be said that Count I of the instant indictment contains more than the bare conclusions of the pleader, having no *videlicet* following.

In particular, can it be said that the Count (i) fairly apprises the defendants of the facts said to constitute a crime with sufficient certainty? (ii) fairly apprised the Grand Jury of the facts said to constitute a crime with sufficient specificity so that we can tell what was in the minds of the Grand Jurors, and more important, whether what was in the minds of the Grand Jurors and what was in the minds of the prosecutors was the same thing? (iii) fairly apprises the Court of whether the facts said to constitute "harboring and concealing" would in fact, if proven, constitute that crime within the limiting language of the cases which have defined harboring and concealing in narrow, restricted terms, rather than in the broadest possible connotation of those words?

For definition and delimitation of the crime, see: *Firpo* v. *United States,* 261 Fed. 850 (2nd Cir. 1919); *United States* v. *Shapiro,* 113 F.2d 891 (2nd Cir. 1940); *United States* v. *Thornton,* 178 F. Supp. 42 (E.D. N.Y. 1959); *United States* v. *Biami,* 243 F. Supp. 917 (E.D. Wis. 1965).

We suggest that all three of the questions must be answered in the negative and that Count I is insufficient and constitutes no more than the conclusion of the pleaders.

In the first place, Count I does not specify the place or places where the alleged harboring and concealing occurred. It states only "at New Shoreham" and over a period of some four days. What was in the minds of the Grand Jury as to place? New Shoreham is approximately 6 miles long by 3½ miles wide. Was the alleged crime committed in several places and in what type of place or places—a closet in a church? A cave or well? A hotel room? If in a home, it would make a difference as to whether it was in a tunnel in the cellar, for example, or in a ground-level room with windows readily open to view. If the latter, would the Grand Jury have indicted if the facts alleged in Count I had so stated?

The omission to allege the place of the crime required dismissal in *Davis* v. *United States,* 357 F.2d 438 (5th Cir. 1966), cert. den. 385 U.S. 927. Count III charged that defendants on two dates, in the southern district of Florida, wilfully attempted to wreck trains of the Florida East Coast Railroad. The court, at page 446, stated:

The language is not specific enough to state a single offense. Count III could refer to the same events which form the basis of the first two indictments, or it could refer to a completely different set of circumstances. The use of the word "trains" and the failure to specify even the approximate location where the attempt took place are particularly objectionable since they subject appellants to unwarranted speculation:

"Undoubtedly the language of the statute may be used in the general description of an offense, but it must be accompanied with such a statement of the facts and circumstances as will inform the accused of the specific offense, coming under the general description, with which he is charged."

Count III should have been dismissed.

Similarly, there is no possible way for defendants here, or the Grand Jury, or the Court, to tell whether Count I and Count II of the instant indictment refer to the same set of circumstances or a completely different set of circumstances. Consequently, the Count is insufficient to "apprise" with certainty.

Carrying this point further as to the omission of any recitation of facts relating to concealment (concealment of fraud, rather than concealment of persons), there is a particularly apt discussion of minimum standards below which an indictment may not descend and still stand in *United States* v. *Harris,* 217 F. Supp. 86 (M.D. Ga. 1962) in which the court relied heavily upon and quoted freely from *Apex Distributing.*

In *Harris,* the charge was that defendant concealed the fact that rolls of paper did not comply with government specifications. The indictment charged concealment in the language of the statute but not the manner or the mode or the acts constituting concealment. The Court, holding the indictment bad, said at page 87:

The indictment recognizes the existence of the three specified essential ingredients of the offense by copying them verbatim from the statute. *This incorporation of statutory language in the indictment is, without more, only a legal conclusion of the pleader.* The draftsman of the indictment doubtless so recognized because, after setting forth the statutory language, he continues, "in the following manner, to wit"; obviously essaying to do what Rule 7(c), Federal Rules of Criminal Procedure requires, namely, set forth a "written statement of the essential facts constituting the offense charged.". . . But we look in vain to the indictment for any "statement of essential facts" showing (1) any concealment or covering up, or (2) any trick, scheme, or device. [Emphasis added]

In our research we have as yet failed to find a case charging "harboring" in violation of 18 U.S.C. §1071 without some particularizing as to the overt acts and circumstances. Few of the harboring decisions are directed to the validity of the indictment. One of those which is so directed offers a striking contrast to the instant indictment in that seven overt acts were alleged following statutory language of harboring, concealing and transporting an alien in violation of the immigration laws. That case was *Reno* v. *United States,* 317 F.2d 499 (5th Cir. 1963). Two of the three judges found the "overt acts" sufficient; the third did not. The dissenter's opinion points up the problem with the instant Count I, i.e., that it has no *videlicet.* At page 506, he said:

We may be sure that all that portion of the indictment which precedes the videlicet or scilicet, "that is to say" amounts to no more than the statement of a legal conclusion. [*United States* v. *Straus,* 283 F.2d 155, 158 n. 6 (5 Cir. 1960)], and is, of course, insufficient to charge any offense. Furthermore, we normally look to what comes after the videlicet or scilicet to see precisely what the writer, here the draftsman of the indictment, here also the Grand Jury, has in mind. "The use of the 'videlicet' is to point out, particularize, or render more specific that which has been previously stated in general language only; also to explain that which is doubtful or obscure" Black, Law Dictionary (4th ed. 1951). "A general expression in an indictment may be restricted and confined to a precise and definite fact by a description under a videlicet or scilicet" *Beauchamp* v. *United States,* 154 F.2d 413, 415 (6 Cir., 1946). We may be sure also that what comes after the "that is to say" does not even point toward a conspiracy, much less allege one, but charges only or at most substantive offenses.

In the light of the above cases, the basic questions under Count I are obvious. Would a Grand Jury have charged an offense had overt acts been recited in the indictment?

Is the Court well enough informed—or indeed informed at all—as to whether the overt acts in fact constitute a crime?

Can the defendants know, in preparing their defense, whether the overt acts believed by the prosecutor to constitute harboring and concealing are any more, or any less, or otherwise different from the acts charged in Count II, namely, giving "sustenance and lodging."

Were the charge "rape" or "robbing a bank," the prosecutor, Grand Jury, judge and defendants would all presumably have in mind a course of conduct fairly well defined and circumscribed by the words, they being relatively specific.

Not so the words "harbor or conceal," particularly where the words appear in the alternative in the statute and have been given a narrow definition by the courts. These words are susceptible of far broader and more generalized interpretation than "rape," "bank robbery," or "passing a counterfeit bill."

One obvious example will suffice as to the use of the word "harbor" if not particularized. Would the word by itself without more necessarily mean the same thing to a prosecutor with a farm or factory background and a grand juror from the merchant marine, recently rescued from shipwreck.

The use of the word "conceal" also may be far from precise and may connote many different types of conduct—unlike a word like "rape" which is a single-meaning word. First there is a question of degree. Concealment may be regarded by some as absolute in degree (the tunnel under the cellar floor), by others as partial or periodic, (e.g., the innkeeper lodging a guest overnight may be "concealing" for that time). The concealment may vary as to its manner—total concealment of the soldier in the trenches; camouflage concealment of the soldier in the open. The furnishing of wigs or disguises may be concealment in one sense, although the disguisee be in plain view.

In the instant case, Count II alleges the overt act of providing "sustenance and lodging." Were these, in the mind of the prosecutor, the same acts contemplated by him as "harboring and concealing" in Count I? More important, were they the acts the Grand Jury considered as the only acts applicable to Count I, or were there other acts?

As *Russell* teaches, subsequent guesses as to what was in the mind of the Grand Jury deprive defendants of a basic protection.

Defendants may not, under our law, be convicted on the basis of facts not found by the Grand Jury—not perhaps even presented to the Grand Jury. 369 U.S. at 770.

We are left under Count I with speculation as to what was in the minds of the Grand Jury; indeed, as to what was in the mind of the prosecutor. This, we respectfully submit, requires that the Count be dismissed.

We attach an appendix of additional cases on the points herein for reference, if any be needed beyond those discussed above.

Respectfully submitted,
By their attorneys,

EDWIN H. HASTINGS
DeWITTE T. KERSH, JR.

Tillinghast, Collins & Graham
1030 Hospital Trust Building
Providence, Rhode Island 02903
(401-274-3800)

January 25, 1971

Appendix

Marshall v. *United States*, 355 F.2d 999 (9th Cir. 1966) on the point that more than a bare-bones indictment is needed (page 1003);

United States v. *Beard*, 414 F.2d 1014 (3d Cir. 1969) on the point that the court cannot be left to guess what was in the minds of the grand jury (page 1016);

United States v. *Borland*, 309 F. Supp. 280 (D. Del. 1970)—in a conspiracy to conceal case, the court quotes at length the *Apex Distributing* opinion;

United States v. *Farinas*, 299 F. Supp. 852 (S.D. N.Y. 1969); especially apropos of the instant case. At page 854:

"Further, where an indictment condemns an act belonging to a species of conduct, which species includes other acts not amounting to indictable offenses, it is not sufficient that the indictment merely identifies the species in general but, rather, it must particularize the act or acts which, it is alleged, constitute the offense charged, . . . so that the court can be assured that the indictment charges conduct which is, in fact, prohibited by law."

Overstreet v. *United States*, 321 F.2d 459 (5th Cir. 1963) cert. den. 376 U.S. 919 (1964), Brown, J., dissenting at page 463: "The vital function of the Grand Jury ought not to be whittled down to extricate prosecutors from the consequences of slovenly draftsmanship."

United States v. *Panzavecchia*, 421 F.2d 440 (5th Cir. 1970). Defendant has a constitutional right to know what "offense" is being charged;

Joyner v. *United States*, 320 F.2d 798 (App. D.C. 1963), Bazelon, J., concurring, pointed to possibility that conviction was based on facts not found by grand jury;

Williams v. *District of Columbia*, 419 F.2d 638 (App. D.C. 1969). The information used statutory language in regard to use of obscene and profane language. The Court required particularization of circumstances noting that a carpenter who misses a nail may and probably will use such language in circumstances not criminal. In the instant case, "harboring" has criminal and noncriminal implications, indeed, it may have commendable, as well as evil, connotations—hence, it must be particularized.

Defendants' Motion to Dismiss Count II

UNITED STATES DISTRICT COURT

FOR THE

DISTRICT OF RHODE ISLAND

UNITED STATES OF AMERICA

v.

WILLIAM STRINGFELLOW and

ANTHONY TOWNE

Indictment No. 7709

Motion to Dismiss

Defendants respectfully move that Count II of the Indictment for alleged violation of 18 U.S.C. §3 ("Accessory after the fact") be dismissed on the following grounds:

1. Count II is defective in that while charging these defendants with being accessories after the fact to "destruction of Government property and wilful interference with the ad-

ministration of the Military Selective Service Act" by their alleged principal, Daniel Berrigan, it does not state when or where the alleged destruction and wilful interference by Daniel Berrigan took place (except that it occurred in the District of Maryland), so that these defendants are unable properly to defend against this charge.

2. Count II is defective in that it does not state that from on or about August 7, 1970, to August 11, 1970, the said Daniel Berrigan was a fugitive.

Defendants further state that without waiving the objections set forth above in support of this Motion to Dismiss, they respectfully move that Count II of the Indictment be dismissed on the following additional grounds:

3. Count II alleges no facts as to any act done by defendants or either of them to hinder or prevent punishment of Daniel Berrigan.

4. The only facts alleged in said Count are allegations that defendants did receive Daniel Berrigan at their residence and did give sustenance and lodging to him, none of which facts separately or in combination constitute prevention or hindrance of punishment.

5. Count II is invalid in that it does not allege facts which constitute one continuous criminal transaction in which these defendants may be charged as accessories after the fact with their alleged principal, Daniel Berrigan, in the single offense of destruction of government property and interference with administration of Selective Service Act.

6. If the offenses alleged to have been committed by the said Daniel Berrigan are presumed to consist of the destruction of government property and the wilful interference with the administration of the Military Selective Service Act on or about May 17, 1968, in Catonsville, Maryland, for which Daniel Berrigan was indicted and stood trial on or about October 7, 1968, in the United States District Court for the District of Maryland, was released until completion of appeal (as to which the

United States Supreme Court finally denied certiorari on February 24, 1970), then Count II is invalid since defendants could not have been charged as accessories in the same indictment with the alleged principal.

7. Count II is invalid in that it alleges no facts stating that defendants or either of them hindered or prevented the "apprehension" and "the trial" of Daniel Berrigan (Daniel Berrigan having voluntarily submitted to immediate arrest at the site of the alleged destruction of government property), and, as it has been construed, Section 3 of 18 U.S.C. has required a hindrance or prevention of apprehension and trial as well as a hindrance of punishment.

8. The "accessory after the fact" statute (18 U.S.C. §3) does not apply where there has been no hindrance or prevention of apprehension and trial, and where the alleged delay in punishment has been proximately caused by intervening action of the United States, which, after Daniel Berrigan voluntarily submitted himself to its custody, could have retained him in custody, but by its own action permitted him to leave such custody.

9. Said Count II is defective in that the offenses alleged to have been committed by Daniel Berrigan, namely, destruction of government property and wilful interference with the administration of the Selective Service Act were, we presume, committed in Catonsville in the District of Maryland on or about May 17, 1968, and the alleged feeding and lodging of Daniel Berrigan by defendants is alleged to have occurred in the District of Rhode Island in August, 1970, at a date or dates so remote in time as to render unreasonable a charge that defendants or either of them were accessories after the fact to such destruction and interference as allegedly occurred more than two years earlier.

10. Count II of said indictment is invalid under the due process of law clause of Article V of Amendments to the Constitution of the United States in its attempt to apply the acces-

sory after the fact statute to alleged crimes of destruction of government property and interference with the Selective Service Act where the alleged accessory acts (a) were humanitarian acts consisting only of giving sustenance and shelter, and (b) were acts so remote in time and place from the alleged principal crime.

11. Said count of said indictment is invalid under the free exercise of religion clause of Article I of Amendments to the Constitution of the United States in its attempt to apply the accessory after the fact statute to alleged crimes of destruction of government property and interference with the Selective Service Act where the alleged accessory acts were religiously compelled and directed acts consisting only of giving sustenance and shelter to a fellow human.

12. Said Count of said indictment is invalid in proscribing action after the alleged principal offense identical in nature to other concededly lawful action after the alleged principal offense. As shown by the annexed affidavit, defendants received Daniel Berrigan and gave him sustenance and lodging at their home on Block Island in the month of August, 1968, in the late spring of 1969, and in August of 1969, all at times after the alleged destruction of government property and interference with the administration of the Selective Service Act, which acts of giving sustenance and lodging on said dates defendants believe to have been lawful even though occurring closer in time to the presumed date of the alleged wrongful acts of Daniel Berrigan than the alleged wrongful giving of sustenance and lodging in August, 1970.

By their attorneys,

EDWIN H. HASTINGS
DEWITTE T. KERSH, JR.

Tillinghast, Collins & Graham
1030 Hospital Trust Building
Providence, Rhode Island 02903
(401-274-3800)

To: Lincoln B. Almond, Esq.

    U.S. Attorney

Please take notice that the undersigned will bring the above motion on for hearing before the United States Court for the District of Rhode Island on February 1, 1971, at 10:00 A.M. or as soon thereafter as counsel can be heard.

EDWIN H. HASTINGS

Certificate of Service

I certify that on January 5, 1971, I served a copy of the foregoing motion upon Lincoln B. Almond, Esq., by delivery to his office.

EDWIN H. HASTINGS

Memorandum of Law

IN THE DISTRICT COURT OF THE UNITED STATES

FOR THE DISTRICT OF RHODE ISLAND

UNITED STATES OF AMERICA

           v.   *Indictment No. 7709*

WILLIAM STRINGFELLOW and

    ANTHONY TOWNE

Memorandum in Support of Defendants'
Motion to Dismiss Count II of the Indictment

1. The first ground for dismissal of Count II is directed at the point that these defendants are being charged with being accessories after the fact to destruction of government property and wilful interference with the administration of the Military Selective Service Act. The Count charges that their alleged principal, Daniel Berrigan, had committed "Offenses"—a plural word.

It appears an elementary proposition of federal criminal law that such a charge in an indictment is insufficient without specifying times and places.

Russell v. *United States,* 369 U.S. 749 (1962). As indicated in *Russell,* the indictment must "sufficiently apprise the defendant of what he must be prepared to meet," (369 U.S. at 763). Also it must contain the elements of the offense with enough specificity so that if other proceedings are taken against him, "he may plead a former acquittal or conviction," (369 U.S. at 764).

There have been numerous instances since the inception of the Vietnam war (and before) of "destruction of government property." Under *Russell* and other cases—e.g., *Van Liew* v. *United States,* 321 F.2d 664 (5th Cir. 1963), defendants are entitled to know *what offense* is charged—to what acts are they charged with being accessory (321 F.2d at 670).

2. The second ground for dismissal of Count II is that it does not state that Daniel Berrigan was a fugitive (let alone stating that defendants knew he was a fugitive). All it states is that Daniel Berrigan had "committed offenses"—at a time or times and place or places unstated.

Without a statement as to Daniel Berrigan's status in August of 1970, Count II of the indictment is broad enough to cover the giving of food and lodging to Daniel Berrigan (a) after a statute of limitations had expired, (b) while released on bail, (c) after service of sentence or payment of fine. Unless a statement as to fugitive status, escape status or the like is included in the allegations, there is no basis for an inference to be drawn (as done in the indictment) that the alleged acts of feeding and lodging were committed by defendants "in order to prevent and hinder his punishment."

3 & 4. As to grounds 3 and 4 for dismissal of Count II, they are to the point that the furnishing of food and lodging, without more (and especially after a time gap of several years—

assuming for argument that the principal offense charged occurred several years prior to alleged furnishing of food and lodging), does not constitute the hindering or preventing of "punishment" so as to make defendants "accessories" to the alleged destruction of government property.

Mere acts of charity which comfort or relieve the alleged "principal" do not constitute the renderers of the charitable acts "accessories after the fact." *Maddox* v. *Commonwealth,* 349 S.W. 2d 686 (Ky. 1961) clearly indicated that acts of charity which may "relieve" or may "comfort" a principal do not make the renderer an accessory where the acts are not of a nature which tend to frustrate the due course of justice.

Without intending to be facetious, justice would have been frustrated had the principal died from starvation before serving his sentence, and the maintaining of the essentials for life may have been more of an aid than a hindrance to justice.

The "assistance" referred to in the accessory statute must involve "some participation in the criminal act" (Manton, J. in *Firpo* v. *United States,* 261 Fed. 850, 853 (2nd Cir. 1919). See also the discussion of Hough, J. concurring on this point in the *Firpo* case, saying ". . . it is a very strict and narrow definition . . . of assistance to say it is any word or act which would render the actor liable as accessory after the fact." (261 Fed. at 854.)

"Charitably supplying the prisoner with food" does not constitute the provider an accessory. *People* v. *Dunn,* 53 Hun. 381, 6 N.Y. Supp. 805, 808 (1889). 16 C. J. p. 139.

See also the various cases cited and discussed below, which indicate that the pattern of acts required to constitute a person an "accessory after the fact" indicate a substantial set of acts designed to help the "principal" effectuate his crime or escape from justice.

Since the "accessories" are subject to fine or imprisonment or both in the amount of one-half of the maximum given the principal, it seems apparent from the cases that a great deal more assistance of active criminal consort nature is required than is present in the facts charged in Count II.

5 & 6. The fifth and sixth grounds for dismissal of Count II are that the acts alleged do not constitute one continuous transaction in which defendants as accessories may be charged in a joint indictment with their principal in the single offense of destruction of government property. This is the thrust of the leading Section 3 case, *Skelly* v. *United States,* 76 F.2d 483 (10th Cir. 1935). In *Skelly* it appeared that George Kelly and Albert Bates had kidnapped Charles Urschel and had demanded and received $200,000 in used $20's as ransom. Berman, Skelly and others had, at Bates's request, exchanged some of the "hot" ransom money for unidentifiable currency. Convictions of Berman and Skelly as accessories were confirmed, the court saying at pp. 487–488:

> "An *accessory* is he who is not the chief actor in the offense, nor present at its performance, but is some way concerned therein, either *before* or *after* the fact committed.". . . "An accessory is one who participates in a felony too remotely to be deemed a principal." *Bishop on Criminal Law* (9th Ed.) vol. 1, §663.
>
> . . . . .
>
> The acts of a principal to a substantive offense and the acts of an accessory after the fact thereto, are one continuous criminal transaction. At common law the principal and accessory after the fact may be jointly indicted and where so indicted they should be charged in one count with but one commencement and one conclusion. Therefore the acts of the two constitute a single offense committed by them jointly, one acting as principal and the other as accessory after the fact.

No such continuous transaction is alleged in Count II. There is no charge that defendants (or any one else) in any way interfered with the apprehension or trial of Daniel Berrigan. There is no charge that defendants, after his conviction, aided him to escape. There are no facts indicating that the alleged giving of food and shelter had any relationship whatever to the alleged principal offense, or in any way was part of one continuous criminal transaction in which in some way these defendants can be charged with sharing in the destruction of government property as accessories to that act.

7. The seventh ground for dismissal of Count II is that the Count alleges acts allegedly done only in order to "prevent" punishment, and alleges no acts done by these defendants or others to hinder apprehension or trial.

The words "apprehension, trial or punishment" are literally disjunctive, just as the words in 18 U.S.C. §1071 "harbor or conceal" are disjunctive. As *United States* v. *Shapiro*, 113 F.2d 891 (2nd Cir. 1940) and *Firpo* v. *United States*, 261 Fed. 850 (2nd Cir. 1919) teach, the words "harbor or conceal" are to be read conjunctively, and as all, or substantially all of the cases involving 18 U.S.C. §3, show, the words there are also generally treated as conjunctive.

The reason would seem to be that, as indicated in *Skelly*, supra, the relationship between the acts of the principal and the acts of the accessory must be a close one.

See among others (involving the three elements of avoidance of apprehension, trial *and* punishment):

United States v. *Carrier*, 344 F.2d 42 (4th Cir. 1965)—accessory after the fact drove principal (bank robber) to airport, bought ticket for principal in accessory's name, gave him accessory's credit cards, assisted in his make-up disguise—all to effectuate the robbery. *Neal* v. *United States*, 102 F.2d 643 (8th Cir. 1939) embezzlement from bank by principal, defendant charged with accessory by reason of concealing proceeds of embezzlement. *Sykes* v. *United States*, 224 F.2d 313 (4th Cir. 1955) accessory aiding bank embezzler to escape apprehension, trial and punishment.

Hiram v. *United States,* 354 F.2d 4 (9th Cir. 1965) accessory drove bank robber from San Francisco to Portland to avoid apprehension and trial as well as punishment.

Orlando v. *United States,* 377 F.2d 667 (9th Cir. 1967) accessory hid bank robbers under the bed of his house, and concealed stolen money in various parts of his house.

All of the above cases, and most of the other "accessory after the fact" cases, involve acts of a cooperative nature performed by an accessory in close proximity to the time of the criminal act. None of them, so far as we have as yet been able to find, involve cases where the principal was apprehended, tried, convicted and pursued appeals through the Circuit Court to the Supreme Court (certiorari denied February 24, 1970, *Mary Moylan, et al.* v. *United States,* 397 U.S. 910) all occurring as intervening acts between the principal offense (destruction of government records) and the alleged acts with which the government now seeks to make these defendants accessories to the earlier destruction of records.

8. The eighth ground for dismissal of Count II is directed at the proximate cause for any delay in the punishment of Daniel Berrigan. The attempt in Count II is to link these defendants with the destruction of government property occurring (presumably) more than two years earlier because of their alleged efforts [by feeding and lodging] to delay the punishment of their alleged principal.

Yet it seems obvious that where the government itself had it in its power to prevent any delay in punishment by retaining the principal in custody—in which event these defendants would not have had an opportunity to feed and lodge the principal, the government's own action, through its federal court in Maryland, in releasing the principal on bail, is an intervening event which should effectively insulate anyone who later fed and lodged the principal from complicity as accessories in the crime of destroying government property.

As averred on oath in the annexed affidavit, these defendants fed and lodged the principal on a number of occasions after the principal crime had been committed on the not unreasonable assumption that since the government had released him, their feeding and lodging him would not make them accessories to the earlier crime.

Indeed, if persons released on bail may not be fed and lodged by friends and relatives after their release on bail without subjecting their friends and relatives to the charge of being accessories after the fact to the principal crime, there is little or no point to the bail release procedure.

9 & 10. The ninth and tenth grounds for dismissal of Count II go to the unreasonableness, to the point of a violation of due process of law, of an attempt by the government to criminally relate acts, through the "accessory" statute, which are so extremely remote in time and place to the principal offense.

Although the indictment does not say so, we presume for this argument that the principal offense occurred at a time and place unstated, but sometime in May of 1968 and some place in Maryland, and the alleged feeding and lodging is said in the indictment to have occurred at Block Island in August of 1970, some two and a quarter years later. Adding to the inherent unreasonableness of the time gap, is the attempt to convert acts which are inherently humanitarian and charitable into acts which are criminal, related through the accessory statute to the principal offense.

Further adding to the inherent unreasonableness of applying the accessory statute to these defendants are the numerous acts of judicial process involving the principal occurring between the principal crimes in May, 1968, and the feeding in August of 1970. In this period the principal (a) voluntarily gave himself up at the time of the crime, (b) appeared promptly for trial, (c) proceeded through an appeal to the Fourth Circuit, 417 F.2d 1002 (Oct. 15, 1969), and (d) petitioned for certiorari to the Supreme Court (denied February 24, 1970, 397 U.S. 910, 25 L. Ed. 2d 91, sub. nom. *Mary Moylan et al.* v. *U.S.*).

We have thus far in our research found no cases approaching a comparable time lag in an attempt by the government to charge a person as an accessory to an earlier crime.

To apply 18 U.S.C. §3 in the circumstances referred to in Count II is, we respectfully suggest, a gross violation of the principal of definiteness in criminal acts, and the basic requirement that an actor, to be criminal, must have a reasonable opportunity to know that his conduct is proscribed.

Thus, as examples and without endeavoring to be exhaustive, see

United States v. *Harris,* 347 U.S. 612 (1954) at p. 617 (Warren, C. J.):

> The constitutional requirement of definiteness is violated by a criminal statute that fails to give a person of ordinary intelligence fair notice that his contemplated conduct is forbidden by the statute. The underlying principle is that no man shall be held criminally responsible for conduct which he could not reasonably understand to be proscribed.

and *Bouie* v. *City of Columbia,* 378 U.S. 347 (1964) (Brennan, J.) at p. 351:

> We have recognized in such cases that "a statute which either forbids or requires the doing of an act in terms so vague that men of common intelligence must necessarily guess at its meaning and differ as to its application, violates the first essential of due process of law," and that "No one may be required at peril of life, liberty or property to speculate as to the meaning of penal statutes."

11. The eleventh ground for dismissal of Count II is that the attempt to apply the accessory statute to make criminal

the acts of providing food and lodging to a fellow human is in violation of the free exercise of religion clause of the First Amendment.

The government will not deny that the context of the principal crime and the alleged accessory crime were committed by Christians, as was the principal crime. (See footnotes 19 and 21 417 F.2d at 1002, opinion of Judge Sobeloff in *United States* v. *Moylan, et al.*

To furnish food and shelter to one's brothers was, for these defendants pursuant to commands set forth in the Bible in many places, see, e.g.:

> After breakfast [at Galilee after the resurrection], Jesus said to Simon Peter, "Simon, son of John, do you love me more than all else?" "Yes, Lord," he answered, "you know that I love you." "Then feed my lambs," he said. (A direction twice more repeated in Jesus' final words) John 21:15–16.
>
> Then the king will say to those on his right hand, "You have my Father's blessing; come, enter and possess the kingdom that has been ready for you since the world was made. For when I was hungry, you gave me food; when thirsty, you gave me drink . . ." Then the righteous will reply, "Lord, when was it that we saw you hungry and fed you, or thirsty and gave you drink . . . ?" And the king will answer, "I tell you this: anything you did for one of my brothers here, however humble, you did for me." Matt. 25:34–40. (From the translation in the New English Bible.)

Any attempt by the government to prohibit these or other defendants from following their religious duty to feed and shelter a fellow human is inhibited by the First Amendment to at least the same degree (if not greater) than the First Amendment proscription against compulsory flag salute [*Board of Education* v. *Barnette,* 319 U.S. 624 (1943)], or licensing ordinances inhibiting persons from selling religious books [*Follett* v. *McCormick,* 321 U.S. 565 (1944)]

12. The twelfth ground for dismissal of Count II is that it purports to proscribe by criminal penalties acts which took place after the alleged principal offense which were identical in nature to other concededly lawful acts occurring after the alleged principal offense.

The charge is that these defendants gave food and lodging to Daniel Berrigan knowing that he had committed the principal offense of destruction of government property. As the affidavit annexed to the motion shows, these defendants gave food and lodging to Daniel Berrigan on one occasion in 1968 and on two occasions in 1969, all three occasions presumably after the principal offense had occurred.

True the indictment alleges that the food and lodging said to have been given in August of 1970 was given with an evil intent; i.e., "in order to prevent and hinder his punishment," but it strains belief that of four occasions of giving food and lodging occurring after the principal offense, the first three should be lawful and the fourth unlawful, and so seriously unlawful as to link these defendants with the original offense as accessories.

Respectfully submitted,

EDWIN H. HASTINGS
DeWITTE T. KERSH, JR.

Tillinghast, Collins & Graham
1030 Hospital Trust Building
Providence, Rhode Island 02903

Supplemental Memorandum

UNITED STATES DISTRICT COURT

FOR THE

DISTRICT OF RHODE ISLAND

UNITED STATES OF AMERICA

v.

WILLIAM STRINGFELLOW and

ANTHONY TOWNE

Indictment No. 7709

Supplemental Memorandum of Defendants
in Regard to Motion to Dismiss Count II

In their supplemental memorandum in regard to Count I, filed January 25, 1971, defendants have cited, quoted or discussed a number of cases in which indictments have been dismissed for lack of particularity in sufficiently apprising the defendants, the grand jury and the court as to what offense is actually charged.

Most of the cases discussed in that memo apply with equal or greater force to the first ground of the motion to dismiss Count II, namely, that the Count does not specify times or places of the alleged principal offenses of destruction of government property and interference with the Selective Service Act.

We call particularly to the Court's attention *Davis* v. *United States,* 357 F.2d 438 (5th Cir. 1966) where the failure to specify even the approximate location of the attempt to wreck a train rendered the indictment invalid (pp. 6–7 of the memo of January 25, 1971).

In connection with Count II's charge that these defendants are accessories to an alleged undated and unplaced destruction of government property by Daniel Berrigan, the Court may take notice that additional charges relating to conspiracy to destroy government property have been brought in the Middle District of Pennsylvania, naming Daniel Berrigan as a co-conspirator, which adds to the uncertainty attendant to the allegations in Count II.

From the form of the indictment in Count II, can the defendants tell, or can the Court tell, what destruction of government property or what interference with the Selective Service Act was in the minds of the Grand Jurors to which they charged these defendants with being accessories.

Respectfully submitted
By their attorneys,

EDWIN H. HASTINGS
DEWITTE T. KERSH, JR.

Tillinghast, Collins & Graham
1030 Hospital Trust Building
Providence, Rhode Island 02903
(401-274-3800)

January 26, 1971

Government's Reply Memorandum

IN THE DISTRICT COURT OF THE UNITED STATES
FOR THE DISTRICT OF RHODE ISLAND

UNITED STATES OF AMERICA

v.

WILLIAM STRINGFELLOW and

ANTHONY TOWNE

Indictment No. 7709

*Reply Memorandum to Defendants'
Motion to Dismiss*

The defendants have filed separate Motions to Dismiss the indictment herein.

As to the Motion relative to Count I, Counsel for defendants rely on *Russell* v. *United States* (369 U.S. 749). The indictment involved therein charged defendants with violating 2 U.S.C. Sec. 192 for refusing to answer "any question pertinent to the question under inquiry" before a Congressional Committee. The indictment failed to state the subject under inquiry before the Committee. The Supreme Court ruled that the indictment should at least identify the subject under inquiry. Obviously this case is in no way factually analogous to the case for which the defendants have been indicted.

The test of sufficiency of an indictment is not whether it could not have been more artfully and precisely drawn, but rather, whether it contains the elements of the offense intended to be charged, sufficiently apprises the defendant of what he must be prepared to meet, and in the event of subsequent proceedings similar to the offense charged whether the record shows with accuracy to what extent the defendant may plead a former acquittal or conviction. *United States* v. *Gallo,* 299 Fed. Supp., 697. *United States* v. *Rezzo,* 418 F.2d, 71. *United States* v. *Messler,* 414 F.2d, 1293. cert. den. 397 U.S., 913.

A reading of Count I, which charges a violation of 18 U.S.C., 1071 (so called "Harboring Statute"), indicates that a certain place (namely "Block Island"), the defendants at a certain time (on or about August 7, 1970), did unlawfully, wilfully and knowingly harbor and conceal, Daniel Berrigan, so as to prevent the apprehension of Daniel Berrigan for whom a warrant had been issued in the District of Maryland. (Obviously Paraphrased.) The Statute (18 U.S.C. 1071 Reads:

> Whoever harbors or conceals any person for whose arrest a warrant or process has been issued under the provisions of any law of the United States, so as to prevent his discovery and arrest, after notice or knowledge of the fact that a warrant or process has been issued for the apprehension of such person, shall be fined not more than $1,000 or imprisoned not more than one year, or both; except that if the warrant or process issued on a charge of felony, or after conviction of such person of any offense, the punishment shall be a fine of not more than $5,000, or imprisonment for not more than five years, or both. As amended Aug. 20, 1954, c. 771, 68 Stat. 747.

The wording of the indictment does more than charge a statutory crime substantially in the words of the statute. It in fact alleges dates, places, and other information necessary to identify the violation. This District Court has repeatedly held that an indictment is sufficient that charges a statutory crime substantially in the words of the statute. *United States* v. *O'Toole,* 101 Fed. Supp., 123. *United States* v. *Catamore Jewelry,* 124 Fed. Supp., 846. *United States* v. *Apex Distributing,* 148 Fed. Supp., 365. The indictment herein covers the elements of the offense charged and apprises the defendant of the nature of the offense so that he can adequately prepare a defense. *United States* v. *Tijerina,* 407 F.2d, 349. cert. den. 396 U.S., 843. *United States* v. *Borland,* 309 Fed. Supp., 280. *United States* v. *DeSapio,* 299 Fed. Supp., 436.

Count II

The arguments propounded relative to Count I above are incorporated herein, with reference to Count II.

Count II charges the defendants with violation of 18 U.S.C. Sec. 3, (Accessory after the fact.)

The Statute reads:

> Whoever, knowing that an offense against the United States has been committed, receives, relieves, comforts or assists the offender in order to hinder or prevent his apprehension, trial or punishment, is an accessory after the fact.
>
> Except as otherwise expressly provided by any Act of Congress, an accessory after the fact shall be imprisoned not more than one-half the maximum term of imprisonment or fined not more than one-half the maximum fine prescribed for the punishment of the principal, or both; or if the principal is punishable by death, the accessory shall be imprisoned not more than ten years.

The indictment charges that the defendants in essence, unlawfully, wilfully and knowingly relieved, received, comforted and assisted Daniel Berrigan in order to prevent and hinder his punishment, relative to certain offenses, enumerated with the indictment. It is obvious and plain on its fact, that this Count related to hindering and preventing the punishment of Daniel Berrigan after he had committed certain acts against the United States Government. It does not in any way say, that the defendants aided Daniel Berrigan in the commission of destruction of Government property or the wilful interference with the administration of the Military Selective Service Act, nor does it allege that the defendants hindered the apprehension of Daniel Berrigan for the commission of the said acts. An indictment need not allege elements which are not essential parts of the offense charged. *United States* v. *Trioli,* 308 Fed. Supp., 358.

The indictment charges the defendants with hindering the *punishment* of Daniel Berrigan, knowing that he in fact did destroy Government property and that he wilfully interfered with the administration of the Military Selective Service Act.

It is not the purpose of an indictment to set forth all the evidence the prosecution will use in presenting its case. It need not anticipate affirmative defenses. *United States* v. *Sisson,* 90 Sup. Court 2117.

An indictment is sufficient if it apprises a defendant of the nature of the charge which he must meet and if its allegations are sufficiently specific to stand as a bar to further prosecution for same offense.

(Citations above)

Respectfully submitted,

LINCOLN C. ALMOND
United States Attorney

EVERETT C. SAMMARTINO
Assistant U.S. Attorney

January 28, 1971

Decision by Chief Judge Edward Day

UNITED STATES OF AMERICA

v.

WILLIAM STRINGFELLOW and

ANTHONY TOWNE

Indictment No. 7709

By his Honor, Chief Judge Day
Tuesday, February 16, 1971

APPEARANCES:

For the Government: Everett C. Sammartino, Assistant United States Attorney

For the Defendants: Tillinghast, Collins & Graham; Edwin H. Hastings, Esq. and DeWitte T. Kersh, Jr., Esq. of counsel.

DECISION

RE DEFENDANTS' MOTION TO DISMISS

THE COURT. (Delivered orally from the bench)

The defendants in this two-count indictment are charged

with harboring and concealing a convicted felon, one Daniel Berrigan, "who had failed to surrender himself at the direction of the Court to commence service of the sentence imposed upon him," (Count I) and with being accessories after the fact to the crimes of Berrigan (Count II), in violation of Title 18, United States Code, Section 2071, and Title 18, United States Code, Section 3, respectively.

The matter is now before me on the defendant's motion to dismiss the indictment in its entirety; that is, to dismiss both Counts I and II.

In support of their motion the defendants urge these grounds:

(1) that the indictment fails to meet the requirements of Rule 7(c) of the Federal Rules of Criminal Procedure "in that it does not state the essential facts constituting the offense charged";

(2) that it violates the Fifth Amendment to the United States Constitution "in that it is not specific enough to insure that it is the indictment of the Grand Jury rather than the indictment of the prosecutor";

(3) that it also violates the Sixth Amendment to the Constitution "in that it does not with reasonable certainty appraise the defendants with the nature of the accusation against them"; and

(4) that it is defective in that it uses only statutory language "and is not accompanied by such a statement of the facts and circumstances as will inform the defendants of the specific offense with which they are charged."

Rule 7(c) of the Federal Rules of Criminal Procedure provides as follows:

> The indictment or the information shall be a plain, concise and definite written statement of the essential facts constituting the offense charged. . . .

The Supreme Court of the United States has emphasized two of the protections which an indictment is intended to guarantee, reflected by two of the criteria by which the sufficiency of an indictment is to be measured. *Russell* v. *United States*, 369 U.S. 749 (1962). At page 763 the Supreme Court held these criteria to be

> . . . first, whether the indictment "contains the elements of the offense intended to be charged, 'and sufficiently apprises the defendant of what he must be prepared to meet,' " and, secondly, " 'in case any other proceedings are taken against him for a similar offence, whether the record shows with accuracy to what extent he may plead a former acquittal or conviction.' *Cochran and Sayre* v. *United States*, 157 U.S. 286, 290; *Rosen* v. *United States*, 161 U.S. 29, 34.". . .

Even before *Russell* v. *United States*, Rule 7(c) was consistently applied to require that "the offense charged must be clearly and accurately alleged in the indictment," since such clarity is compelled by the Sixth Amendment to the Constitution. *United States* v. *Lamont*, 18 F.R.D. 27, 30, S.D. N.Y. (1955).

In short, the indictment must, in addition to reciting the statute allegedly violated, "indicate the manner in which the alleged violation occurred and the essential factual allegations in support thereof." *United States* v. *Levinson*, 405 F.2d 971, 977, 6 Cir. (1968).

It is true that statutory language may be employed in the indictment but

> . . . It is not sufficient to charge an offense in the words of the statute creating it, unless such words themselves, without uncertainty, set forth all essential elements to constitute the crime intended to be punished.

United States v. *Simplot*, 192 F. Supp. 734, 737, D.C. Utah (1961).

The indictment may not use words which might refer to different activities—*Davis* v. *United States,* 357 F.2d 438, 5 Cir. (1966)—and where there are several forms or species of a particular violation, the indictment "must allege the essential facts of the species charged." *Mims* v. *United States,* 332 F.-2d 944, 946, 10 Cir. (1964).

In Count I the defendants are charged with "harboring and concealing," language employed in the statute. This Court has consistently held that particulars of an alleged crime must be stated in an indictment which relies upon a statute which employs broad and comprehensive language descriptive of the general nature of the offense. See *United States* v. *Apex Distributing Company,* 148 F. Supp. 365, 371, D.C. R.I. (1957).

In *United States* v. *Cruikshank,* 92 U.S. 542, 558 (1875), the Supreme Court said:

> . . . It is an elementary principle of criminal pleading that where the definition of an offence, whether it be at common law or by statute, "includes generic terms, it is not sufficient that the indictment shall charge the offence in the same generic terms as in the definition; but it must state the species—it must descend to particulars.". . .

This principle has been consistently applied to require specificity in an indictment based upon such statutes. See, for example, *United States* v. *Borland,* 309 F. Supp. 280, 287, D.C. Del (1970); *United States* v. *Farinas,* 299 F. Supp. 852. S.D. N.Y. (1969).

The *Cruikshank* case was cited in *Flying Eagle Publications, Inc.* v. *United States,* 273 F.2d 799, 802, 1 Cir. (1960), as being the test which has been applied in this Circuit. This test has been neither changed nor weakened by the *Russell* case. But in my opinion the two cases are complementary in spelling out the requirements of an indictment insofar as specificity is concerned.

In my opinion Count I does not meet the test laid down in *Russell* for it fails to adequately advise the defendants of what they must be prepared to meet. Likewise, in my opinion it does not set forth with reasonable particularity the acts and intent as mandated by the Supreme Court in *United States* v. *Cruikshank,* supra.

In Count I the defendants are charged with "harboring and concealing." No specific overt acts are alleged to identify their so-called criminal acts. Speaking of the statutory use of the words, "harbor and conceal," Judge Swan said in *United States* v. *Shapiro,* 113 F.2d 891, 892–3, 2 Cir. (1940):

> . . . These are active verbs, which have the fugitive as their object. This was recognized by this court in *Firpo* v. *United States,* 2 Cir., 261 F. 850, 851, . . . (where) Judge Manton, writing for the majority, said at page 853 of 261 F.: "To conceal, as used, means to hide, secrete, or keep out of sight. To harbor, as used, means to lodge, to care for, after secreting the deserter." . . . To pay money to a fugitive so that he may shelter, feed or hide himself is not within the accepted meanings of to "harbor or conceal" him.

In short, in my opinion it is clear that the words, "harbor and conceal," must be contsrued narrowly not to include all forms of assistance. *United States* v. *Foy,* 416 F.2d 940, 941, 7 Cir. (1964). That being so, it seems to me that Count I is fatally deficient in that it fails to specify the acts of the defendants for which the Government seeks to hold them criminally responsible. Likewise, the failure of Count I to specify "with reasonable particularity" the place of the defendants' allegedly criminal acts, more than to identify the place as "New Shoreham, commonly known as Block Island," is fatally deficient.

In *United States* v. *Tomasetta,* 429 F.2d 978, 980, 1 Cir. (1970), the indictment was dismissed although it specified the date and city where the alleged crime was committed. The Court said at page 980:

> . . . The federal system views the grand jury as an important element of the criminal process. It, and it alone, is competent to charge an accused with a crime of this nature, as is most vividly illustrated by the rule barring substantive amendments to indictments without resubmission to the grand jury and the fact that a defective indictment is not cured by a bill of particulars. *Russell* v. *United States,* supra n. 2, 369 U.S. at 770–771, 82 S. Ct. 1038. On an indictment as vague as that at bar, it is possible, however unlikely, for a prosecutor to obtain a conviction based wholly on evidence of an incident completely divorced from that upon which the grand jury based its indictment. The prosecution may not have the power "to roam at large" in this fashion. *Russell* v. *United States,* supra n. 2, at 768–771, 82 S. Ct. 1038; *United States* v. *Agene,* 302 F. Supp. 1258, 1261 (S.D. N.Y. 1969) .

In the light of the clear guidelines enunciated by the Supreme Court of the United States and, more recently, again enunciated by the Court of Appeals for this Circuit, I feel constrained to conclude that Count I is legally insufficient and that the defendants' motion to dismiss as to Count I must be granted.

As to Count II the defendants have addressed a similar motion to dismiss on 12 distinct grounds. The Court feels it is unnecessary to consider each of these grounds in detail. It is its considered judgment that this count likewise must be held to be defective because of its insufficiency to comply with the standards which the Court discussed with respect to Count I.

Count II, which must be viewed separately and distinctly from Count I and any of the allegations contained therein, charges the defendants with a violation of Title 18, United States Code, Section 3. That section reads in pertinent part as follows:

Accessory after the fact

Whoever, knowing that an offense against the United States has been committed, receives, relieves, comforts or assists the offender in order to hinder or prevent his apprehension, trial or punishment, is an accessory after the fact.

In its memorandum submitted in opposition to the instant motion to dismiss the Government contends that it seeks to prosecute the defendants only for hindering the punishment of the said Berrigan, and expressly rejects any application of Section 3 of Title 18 insofar as it relates to the hindrance of apprehension or trial.

The defendants contend that the count is deficient in that it fails to state that said Berrigan was a fugitive from justice at the time the defendants allegedly assisted him in order to hinder his punishment.

In my opinion the omission of such an allegation in this count is a very vital omission. All of the decided cases which I have found dealing with said Section 3 have involved the hindering of apprehension and trial of the alleged offender rather than, as here, the hindering of his punishment only.

Viewing the allegations of Count II in the light most favorable to the Government, it appears that the Grand Jury charges that the offender Berrigan was to be punished for his criminal acts and that the defendants hindered punishment.

There is no allegation in Count II that Berrigan was a fugitive at the time of the alleged acts of the defendants in giving him food and lodging.

Absent an allegation that Berrigan was a fugitive from justice at the time of the commission of said acts of feeding or furnishing lodging, such acts, which must be viewed solely on the basis of the record, would obviously be permissible in a post-trial situation where a particular defendant was at liberty on bail pending an appeal, for example.

There should have been an allegation in my opinion in

this particular count that Berrigan, at the time he was given food and lodging—if he was given food and lodging—was in fact a fugitive from justice and was known by the defendants to be a fugitive from justice.

As I indicated with respect to Count I, a count in an indictment must be sufficiently definite to make certain that a prosecutor cannot obtain a conviction for the commission of acts or on grounds different from those presented to and considered by the Grand Jury. *United States* v. *Tomasetta*, supra.

On the face of Count II of this indictment it cannot be said with certainty that evidence was presented to the Grand Jury to the effect that the defendants knew of Berrigan's fugitive status or that the Grand Jury considered the question of the existence of knowledge of that status, if it existed on the part of the defendants.

I reiterate the allegations of Count II must be considered entirely separate and apart from the allegations contained in Count I. Each of these counts charges a separate and distinct offense against the laws of the United States and must stand or fall upon the sufficiency of the allegations of each of them.

Count II merely alleged that the defendants knew that Berrigan had committed certain offenses, and it is to these offenses that the defendants are alleged to be accessories. It is the Government's contention that the allegation in this count of the existence of intent on the part of the defendants to hinder the punishment of Berrigan is sufficient to imply guilty knowledge on their part. I am inclined to disagree with this contention. Not only may inferences not correct fatal omissions— *Harris* v. *United States*, 104 F.2d 41, 8 Cir. (1939)—but "if the facts alleged may all be true and yet constitute no offense, the indictment is insufficient." 41 Am. Jur. 2d Section 70, pp. 919–920, citing *Fleisher* v. *United States*, 302 U.S. 218 (1937) (per curiam).

Even assuming for the sake of argument that the defendants

knew that Berrigan had committed the offenses described in the indictment and gave food and lodging to Berrigan but were not aware that on August 7, 1970, he was not still properly free on bail, they would have committed no offense. It is a necessary allegation that the defendants had knowledge that Berrigan at the time they are alleged to have received him was a fugitive from justice.

A similar situation was dealt with by Judge Manton in *Firpo* v. *United States,* 261 F. 850, 852, 2 Cir. (1919), wherein the defendant was charged with assisting an Army deserter to evade the authorities. In that case the indictment did not charge the defendant with knowledge that the individual was a deserter. But the defendant's conviction was reversed on appeal because the evidence failed to establish such knowledge. In discussing the defendant-lawyer's advice to his client to stay away from his home and from the authorities, Judge Manton said at page 852:

> . . . There is testimony that a representation was made to the attorney that the soldier was home on sick leave and could not return to his duties. Indeed, the soldier testified that he only became a deserter from the time he visited the lawyer. Without knowledge of the fact of a desertion, there could not be said to be a criminal intent to assist Shillace.
>
> To assist, as used in the statute, implies guilty knowledge and felonious intent; knowledge of the wrongful purpose of the deserter. To assist, after such knowledge and intent, is serving the purpose of the deserter. It encourages him and aids him, and thus the offense may be committed. To assist, like to abet, involves some participation in the criminal act.

In my opinion Count II of this indictment is deficient in that it does not within the four corners of that count allege knowledge on the part of the defendants requisite to a proper charge of assisting, as used within the statute involved. More than that, Count II fails to recite that the said Berrigan was in fact a fugitive from justice on or about August 7, 1970. In my opinion the failure of Count II to contain these allegations renders that count deficient under the standards which I more particularly set forth in my discussion as to the sufficiency of Count I.

Accordingly, the defendants' notion to dismiss Count II of the indictment must be and is granted.

I hereby certify that the foregoing 14 pages are a true and accurate transcript according to my stenographic notes.

Official court reporter

EPILOGUE

A LETTER TO DANIEL AND PHILIP
BERRIGAN FROM WILLIAM
STRINGFELLOW AND ANTHONY TOWNE

*More or less concurrent with the Stringfellow-Towne indict-
ment and subsequent dismissal has been the utterance of
further charges involving the Berrigan brothers and other
citizens. After the dismissal of charges against them, the authors
addressed a letter, here published in epilogue, to the brothers
in Danbury prison, having to do with the Harrisburg charges,
as well as a continuing concern for conscientious witness in
this country.*

Eschaton
Block Island, Rhode Island

The Fourth Sunday in Lent, 1971

The Rev. Daniel Berrigan, S.J.
The Rev. Philip Berrigan, S.S.J.
Federal Prison
Danbury, Connecticut

Dear Brothers in Christ,

We who have the gratuitous distinction to be The Block Island Two salute you, and assure you that—even as our hospitality to one of you last summer was not a matter of crime but of love—so our recent relief from indictment is a sign to people of good will and lively hope that reason can still prevail, justice can be redeemed, moral sanity can be recovered, peace can be achieved, conscience can be honored.

If the dismissal of charges against us be a good omen, we have nonetheless received much advice—ominous in another sense—to the effect that we must now be silent about what was done to us (at least until the statute of limitations is tolled) and, more than that, that each of us should be quiet about public affairs (at least until the outcome of the prospective presidential campaign) lest any remarks of ours which the authorities hear, or overhear, incite official reprisal.

Innocent, as we are, of the dismissed charges, or of any offense, we have suffered such opinion with dismay, We are reluctant to endorse so caustic and despairing appraisal of the present administration as a capricious, fantasizing, morally ruthless government. Whatever characterization of the incumbent regime is appropriate, those who urge us to lapse into quietism have reached, we think, a backward conclusion. We cannot live worthily as human beings in fear of official harassment. We cannot forfeit our minds or turn off our consciences just because of real or supposed threats of persecution. To do so would be moral suicide.

We will not simply abdicate our citizenship, nor will we abandon the practice of the Gospel. We will not quit as human beings.

Let somebody else quit.

If repression be so much a reality, let somebody else quit.

Let Dr. Kissinger resign; let Mr. Hoover step aside; let General Westmoreland be discharged; let all spies, informers, wiretappers, undercover agents, secret policemen, as well as assorted birdwatchers, be fired; let the President quit—even as his predecessor did.

Those who warn us to "play it safe" by practicing quietism are not alone in betraying fear of the authorities. Throughout our ordeal we have been astonished to hear ourselves described as courageous. We do not think that an apt description, for we have not only known ourselves to be innocent of an offense but we have considered ourselves to be innocuous—mustering occasional verbal protests against the barbarism in Indochina and the demoralization of society at home, and, in last summer's hospitality, honoring friendship and the faith in an ordinary and customary way. That such should be esteemed as audacious or brave strikes us as an even more remarkable measure of a widespread apprehension with which very many Americans behold the incumbent government than is exposed by those who confess their own fear by advising us to be silent and acquiescent.

It is always characteristic of oppressive societies that fear reigns between regime and people—and not just on the part of the people, but also on the side of the State. Americans have been suffering an administration which is manifestly afraid of its own citizens—afraid of the young, afraid of the blacks, afraid of the poor; afraid of free speech, afraid of free media, afraid of any doubt about its version of events; afraid of ideas, afraid of truth; afraid of persons who think; afraid of nonconformity, afraid of dissent, afraid of citizens who behave as free men.

Sometimes, lately, this extraordinary anxiety in the government has issued in the utterance of ill-founded official charges against citizens who are not docile, which have the effect at once of intimidating other citizens at large and of so pre-occupying the accused in defending themselves that their social dissent is quashed. In our own situation we are experiencing something of this in the trauma and exhaustion of time and money and health ensuing from indictment alone.

But if that be so in a matter like ours, the procurement of the Harrisburg indictment must be said to reveal official anxiety in ferocious proportions. The reality of fear between government and people impinges crucially, in the Harrisburg case, on the matter of credibility. You and the others accused or named have stated your innocence. We believe that. We do not believe the government. We believe you because we know you as men of truth and integrity. We observe that the incumbent authorities, for all their solemnity, have a poor record for candor and a bad reputation for veracity.

Such events as these take place, of course, in a bizarre atmosphere heavy with suspicion, distortion, and peculiar emotion. The official contempt for truth is breathtaking. At a time when you, among the most notorious pacifists in the land, are being accused as terrorists, a President is simultaneously defending his moral commitment to violence in the invasion of Laos while styling himself a "dedicated pacifist."

The incident has a context, of course, in a much longer, more sustained effort mounted during the past several years in which the authorities have sought to inculcate the impression that any dissent is equivalent to violence, thus supposedly justifying harsh action against dissenters. You know better than anyone that that is part of the Catonsville story. The government failed then to comprehend Catonsville as a liturgical event—projecting and applying the promise of the renewal of society which is inherent in all biblical liturgy—and as an action only incidentally, and quite unconventionally, criminal. That could have been recognized in the prosecution of the Catonsville Nine, so that, though you would not have been acquitted, the essential liturgical character of the witness would have been respected, the priority of conscience would have been acknowledged, and the right of dissent in this society would have been protected. Instead, the State proceeded, anxiously, as if a crime of great magnitude had been committed. And now, that same official incapacity, either to comprehend the Christian way or to allow dissent to be viable, culminates in the Harrisburg accusations.

Meanwhile, for those, ourselves among them, committed to nonviolence, there has been a very difficult tactical crisis. Fear is rampant. Intimidation has had success. Many citizens have the impression that any dissent is equivalent to violence, though some of them also suppose that any violence—physical or psychological—done by the State is proper by definition. In such macabre circumstances, what can men do?

In the immediate aftermath of the dismissal of the charges against us, a great number of persons have addressed that question to us. We do not have a grand or an easy or a simple or a short response. We cannot conceive of any response which does not involve the risk of death. Yet we can foresee an end to the tactical paralysis that has bewildered and immobilized so many Americans of concern and conscience up to now, arising directly from the propitious coincidence, in time and as to issues, between the Harrisburg prosecution and the presidential campaign.

The two events are inextricable, and if that fact furnishes

temptations for further abuses of due process of law or for usurpation of the electoral process, it also provides fresh opportunities for citizens to oppose and repudiate the emergent totalitarianism and to act for the renewal of the nation.

That means, as it seems to us, that the demand to end the war now is, both practically and symbolically, an urgent and overwhelming necessity. That cause is potentially decisively augmented both by the enfranchisement of multitudes of younger voters and by the multiplying disillusionment of the so-called middle Americans with the whole war enterprise.

The war must end completely. Not only must the troops be returned, and not only must the prisoners of war be recovered, but those who have been driven into exile must be welcomed home in amnesty.

What has gone wrong in America must be, so far as it can be, rectified, and it is part of that necessity that the cases of those who have been imprisoned, where there is any hint or implication of political prosecution, must be reviewed and rendered subject to executive pardon.

At the same time, precaution against abuse of citizens and of their most elementary rights requires an end of political surveillance, reliance upon informers, resort to entrapment, and the like.

And, in this specific Harrisburg matter, of basic importance is a guarantee to those accused and named of the fullest opportunity to ready their defense and of a scrupulously fair trial. Rudimentary fairness would be served and the prejudicial manner in which the accusations were uttered would be partially allayed, we suggest, if the Director of the FBI were furloughed or suspended, pending the disposition of the case.

We consider that all of these issues are pertinent in both the impending trial and the prospective campaign. That coincidence can end the time of quiescence, frustration, fatigue, indifference, and fear which has so afflicted so many citizens so long.

Dear friends, if we write to you now to assure you of our good morale and of our determination not to succumb to fear and not to become mute, and if by this means we hope to literally encourage our fellow citizens, we also by this letter to you recognize the sense in which the events that engulf all of us can be construed properly and, indeed, profoundly as an offense against the Gospel of Jesus Christ and an aggression by the public authorities against the practice of the Gospel appropriately reminiscent of the anguish and conflict endured by Christians in the Apostolic Church and in subsequent times. This is not a recollection which we make in order to scandalize anyone, nor is it one we make to puff you up or to boast. Rather, we mention these comparable circumstances because, in America now, the war itself, the reality of fear, the temptation to silence, the contempt for reason, the paralysis of conscience—all of these, and more—are in truth ways in which death itself is enshrined as the moral purpose of society, as an idol.

We gladly confess that the resurrection means freedom from idolatry of death.

Thus, when Saint Paul was accused and was brought from his prison cell before the authorities, he said: "With respect to the resurrection of the dead I am on trial before you this day." (Acts 24.21b)

We believe the same plea is yours.